IF I WERE
ANOTHER

MAHMOUD DARWISH

TRANSLATED FROM THE ARABIC
BY FADY JOUDAH

IF I WERE ANOTHER

mahmoud DARWISH

IF I WERE ANOTHER

TRANSLATED FROM THE ARABIC BY FADY JOUDAH

FARRAR STRAUS GIROUX *New York*

FARRAR, STRAUS AND GIROUX

18 West 18th Street, New York 10011

Distributed in Canada by D&M Publishers, Inc.

Printed in the United States of America

First edition, 2009

Grateful acknowledgment is made to the following publications, in which some of these poems originally appeared: *Callaloo*: "A Horse for the Stranger"; *Harvard Review*: "The 'Red Indian's' Penultimate Speech to the White Man"; *Modern Poetry in Translation*: "Like a Hand Tattoo in the Jahili Poet's Ode"; *New American Writing*: "Counterpoint"; *PN Review*: "Rubaiyat," "Truce with the Mongols by the Holm Oak Forest," and "A Music Sentence"; *Poetry Review*: "Tuesday and the Weather Is Clear"; *A Public Space*: "On the last evening on this earth"; *The Threepenny Review*: "Take Care of the Stags, Father"; *Tin House*: "A Canaanite Rock in the Dead Sea"; *Two Lines*: "Rita's Winter." A portion of the introduction was originally published in *The Threepenny Review*.

Library of Congress Cataloging-in-Publication Data

Darwish, Mahmud.

    [Poems. English. Selections]

    If I were another / Mahmoud Darwish ; translated by Fady Joudah.— 1st ed.

      p. cm.

    Includes bibliographical references and index.

    ISBN-13: 978-0-374-17429-3 (hardcover : alk. paper)

    ISBN-10: 0-374-17429-6 (hardcover : alk. paper)

    I. Joudah, Fady, 1971– II. Title.

PJ7820.A7 A215 2009

892.7'16—dc22

2009011521

Designed and typeset by Quemadura

www.fsgbooks.com

1 3 5 7 9 10 8 6 4 2

The translator would like to thank Jonathan Galassi, Louise Glück, Marilyn Hacker, and the editors of the journals in which the above poems first appeared.

CONTENTS

INTRODUCTION *Mahmoud Darwish's Lyric Epic*

hen Mahmoud Darwish and I met on August 4, 2008, five days be-
fore he underwent the surgery that would end his life, he reiterated
the centrality and importance *Mural* holds for this collection. In
Mural he grasped what he feared would be his last chance to write after surviving
cardiovascular death for the second time in 1999. The poem was a song of praise
that affirms life and the humanity not only of the marginalized Palestinian but
also of the individual on this earth, and of Mahmoud Darwish himself. *Mural* was
made into a play by the Palestinian National Theatre shortly after its publication
in 2000 without any prompting from Darwish (his poetry has often been set to
film, music, and song). The staged poem has continued to tour the world to as-
tounding acclaim, in Paris, Edinburgh, Tunisia, Ramallah, Haifa, and elsewhere.
A consummate poet at the acme of innermost experience, simultaneously per-
sonal and universal, between the death of language and physical death, Darwish
created something uniquely his: the treatise of a private speech become collec-
tive. *Mural* was the one magnum opus of which he was certain, a rare conviction
for a poet who reflects on his completed works with harsh doubt equal only to his
ecstatic embrace when on the threshold of new poems.

His first experience of death, in 1984, was peaceful and painless, filled with "whiteness." The second was more traumatic and was packed with intense visions. *Mural* gathered Darwish's experiences of life, art, and death, in their white serenity and violent awakening, and accelerated his "late style" into prolific, progressively experimental output in search of new possibilities in language and form, under the shadow of absence and a third and final death. "Who am I to disappoint the void / who am I," ask the final lines of *The Dice Player*, Darwish's last uncollected lyric epic, written weeks before his death on August 9, 2008. But I still remember his boyish, triumphant laugh when I said to him: "*The Dice Player* is a distilled *Mural* in entirely new diction," and his reply: "Some friends even call it the *anti-Mural*." He had overcome his own art (and death) for one last time, held it apart from himself so that it would indisputably and singularly belong to him and he to it.

If I Were Another is a tribute to Darwish's lyric epic, and to the essence of his "late style," the culmination of an entire life in dialogue that merges the self with its stranger, its other, in continuous renewal within the widening periphery of human grace. The two collections of long poems that begin this book, *I See What I Want* (1990) and *Eleven Planets* (1992), mark the completion of Darwish's middle period. In them he wove a "space for the jasmine" and (super)imposed it on the oppressive exclusivity of historical and antinomian narrative. In 1990, between the personal and the collective, "birth [was] a riddle," but in 1996 birth became "a cloud in [Darwish's] hand." And by *Mural*'s end (2000), there was "no cloud in [his] hand / no eleven planets / on [his] temple." Instead there was the vowel in his name, the letter *Wāw*, "loyal to birth wherever possible." By 2005, Darwish would return, through the medium or vision of almond blossoms, the flower of his birth in March, to revisit the memory and meaning of place, and the "I" in place, through several other selves, in *Exile*, his last collected long poem. Dialectic, lyric, and drama opened up a new space for time in his poetry, a "lateness" infused with age and survival while it does not "go gentle into that good night."

It is necessary to read Darwish's transformation of the long poem over the most accomplished fifteen years of his life: the shift in diction from a gnomic and highly metaphoric drive to a stroll of mixed and conversational speech; the paradoxes between private and public, presence and absence; the bond between the individual and the earth, place, and nature; the illumination of the contemporary Sufi aesthetic method as the essence of poetic knowledge, on the interface of reason and the sensory, imagination and the real, the real and its vanishing where the "I" is interchangeable with (and not split from) its other; and his affair with dialogue and theater (tragic, absurd, or otherwise) to produce a lyric epic sui generis. If Darwish's friend the great critic Edward Said had a leaning toward the novel, Darwish was undoubtedly a playwright at heart. This had been evident since his youth, whether in poems like A *Soldier Dreams of White Lilies* (written in 1967 and now a part of the Norwegian live-film-performance *Identity of the Soul* [2008], in which Darwish is featured) or *Writing to the Light of a Rifle* (1970), or in his brilliant early prose book and its title piece, *Diaries of Ordinary Sorrow* (1973).

Yet Darwish was never comfortable with looking back at his glorious past. He was an embodiment of exile, as both existential and metaphysical state, beyond the merely external, and beyond metaphor, in his interior relations with self and art. Naturally, and perhaps reflexively, Darwish expressed a fleeting reservation at my desire to include here the two older volumes *I See What I Want* and *Eleven Planets*. True, the two are linked to a larger historical reel than is *Mural* or *Exile*, since the former volumes were written during the first Palestinian Intifada, which began in 1987, a major defining event in the identity and hopes of a dispossessed people, and in response to the spectacle of the peace accords Darwish knew would follow. But more important, in these two volumes Darwish had written his *Canto General*, his *Notebook of a Return to My Native Land*, his *Omeros*, destabilizing the hegemony of myth into an inclusive, expansive humanizing lyric that soars, like a hoopoe, over a Canaanite reality and an Andalusian song, where vision is both Sufi and Sophoclean, and elegy arches over the father, the lover, and the other, as well as over a grand historical narrative and its liminal stages on this earth.

I See What I Want and *Eleven Planets* are collections concerned with vision, not image. Even their titles read as one. In the first instance of seeing, Darwish declares a singular self that creates its private lexicon of sorrow and praise and transformation into the collective: a prebiblical past, a Palestinian present, and a future where the self flies "just to fly," free from "the knot of symbols," to where compassion is "one in the nights" with "one moon for all, for both sides of the trench." In *Eleven Planets*, the self has vanished into its other, more elegiacally, and "flight" has reached 1492, the year of "the Atlantic banners of Columbus" and "the Arab's last exhalation" in Granada. The self is transfigured into "The 'Red Indian's' Penultimate Speech" and into "murdered Iraq," this most contemporary of graves, "O stone of the soul, our silence!" Throughout the two books, the oscillation between the "I" and the "we," the private and the public, is maintained in tension, in abeyance. And by the end, Darwish questions himself and his aesthetic: "The dead will not forgive those who stood, like us, perplexed / at the edge of the well asking: Was Joseph the Sumerian our brother, our / beautiful brother, to snatch the planets of this beautiful evening from him?" It is the same beautiful Joseph (son of Jacob) who saw "eleven planets, the sun, and the moon prostrate before [him]" in the Quran, and it is the same past-future elegy of exile and expulsion, circling around to those other sadly beautiful planets "at the end of the Andalusian scene." Yet Darwish triumphs over the void with song: "O water, be a string to my guitar" and "open two windows on shadow street" because "April will come out of our sleep soon" "with the first almond blossom."

I See What I Want marks the first mature presence of the Sufi aesthetic in Darwish's oeuvre, where he will disassemble and reassemble his language, again and again, in an idea of return: wind, horse, wheat, well, dove, gazelle, echo, holm oak, anemones, chrysanthemum, or something more recognizably biographical, like "prison" in Israeli jails. In this recurrence and retreatment, in seating and unseating absence, Darwish is a prodigal between memory and history who extroverts language and the "need to say: Good Morning." Through the process, he attains illumination, not as a fixed and defined state but as the arrival at one truth constantly examined and replaced with another. "Take Care of the Stags, Father" is an elegy to his father, where the father, the "I," the grandfather, and the forefather intertwine and dissolve time, place, and identity "like anemones that adopt the land and sing her as a house for the sky." The private and psychological detail is abundant: Darwish's grandfather was his primary teacher; his father became an endlessly broken man who toiled as a hired laborer on land he owned before the creation of Israel in 1948; the horse he left behind "to keep the house company" when they fled was lost; and the "cactus" that grows on the site of each ruined Palestinian village punctures the heart.

All these details and themes and more are a personal representation first and foremost. Yet the echo resounds a larger collective memory, Palestinian or otherwise. Darwish's fathers resembled, "by chance," the fathers of hundreds of thousand others, and his "I" also resembled another's. History is broken with an earth that "cracks its eggshell and swims between us / green beneath the clouds." And "exile" is "a land of words the pigeons carry to the pigeons," just as the self is "an exile of incursions speech delivers to speech." And the poem is ever present: "Why," "What good is the poem? / It raises the ceiling of our caves and flies from our blood to the language of doves." "Take Care of the Stags, Father" is also a praise for "chrysanthemum," an account of Darwish's profound relationship with the earth, where a different "specificity" and "dailiness" is filtered, captured, through presence and absence. Darwish was a "green" poet whose verse was shaped by flowers, trees, and animals the way people see them: "without story / the lemon blossom is born out of the lemon blossom"; as well as through the dispossessed landscape: a "return" within and without "progress."

The beautifully measured exegesis of "Truce with the Mongols by the Holm Oak Forest," and its epiphora of "holm oak," confirms the formal, thematic, and structural range in these two collections. The mesmerizing prescience in "Truce," however, is alarming. Peace is able to envision itself but, like Cassandra or Tiresias, is either punished or discredited. Thus "The Tragedy of Narcissus the Comedy of Silver" follows in monumental footsteps. Whether in its several stanzaic forms, as an early precursor of *Mural*, or in its undulation between elegy and praise, history and myth, absurdity and distress, this epic must be read with attention to its ubiquitous nuance, its "Ulysses / of paradox," its "Sufi [who] sneaks away from a woman" then asks, "Does the soul have buttocks and a waist and a shadow?" Circumstantially, as noted, the poem is linked to the birth of the first Palestinian Intifada, "a stone scratching the sun." And if this "stone radiating our mystery" will provide fodder for many, "for both sides of the trench," who are drawn to the "political" in Darwish's poetry and life, Darwish offers a reply: "Extreme clarity is a mystery." Darwish wrote not a manifesto for return but a myth of return—where the exiles and displaced "used to know, and dream, and return, and dream, and know, and return, / and return, and dream, and dream, and return." "Bygones are bygones": "they returned / from the myths of defending citadels to what is simple in speech." "No harm befell the land" despite those who "immortalized their names with spear or mangonel . . . and departed," since "none of them deprived April of its habits." "And land, like language, is inherited." And exile is "the birds that exceed the eulogy of their songs." Yet "victims don't believe their intuition" and don't "recognize their names." "Our history is their history," "their history is our history." Darwish asks if anyone managed to fashion "his narrative far from the rise of its antithesis and heroism" and answers: "No one." Still he pleads, "O hero within us ... don't rush," and "stay far from us so we can walk in you toward another ending, the beginning is damned."

Such an ending would find itself in "The Hoopoe." (And just as the two volumes *I See What I Want* and *Eleven Planets* are twins, "The Tragedy of Narcissus the Comedy of Silver" and "The Hoopoe" are twins.) Both poems are tragedies in verse. Threading the dream of return, "The Hoopoe" suspends arrival right from the start: "We haven't approached the land of our distant star yet." And despite the incessant remonstrance and the litany of pretexts by the collective voice in wandering—"Are we the skin of the earth?" "No sword remains that hasn't sheathed itself in our flesh"—the hoopoe insists on simply guiding to "a lost sky," to "vastness after vastness after vastness," and urges us to "cast the place's body" aside, because "the universe is smaller than a butterfly's wing in the courtyard of the large heart." "The Hoopoe" is based on the twelfth-century Sufi narrative epic poem *Conference of the Birds*, by Farid Addin al-Attar of Nishapur. In it a hoopoe leads all birds to the One, who turns out to be all the birds who managed to complete the journey and reach attainment. There are seven wadis on the path to attainment, the last of which is the Wadi of Vanishing, whose essence is Forgetfulness (a visible theme in Darwish's "late" poems). Darwish transforms this Sufi doctrine about God as an internal and not an external reality, a self inseparable from its other, to address exile and the (meta)physicality of identity in a work that is nothing short of a masterpiece.

Similarly, "Eleven Planets at the End of the Andalusian Scene" and "The 'Red Indian's' Penultimate Speech to the White Man" are two of Darwish's most accomplished and beloved poems. The former commemorates five hundred years of the brutal cleansing of Muslims and Jews from Spain, then leaps toward another annihilation across the Atlantic in the latter (which was excerpted and enacted in Jean-Luc Godard's movie *Notre Musique*). In both poems Darwish writes against the perpetual crimes of humans against humanity and against the earth, with the hope these crimes won't be repeated. Darwish clings to the dream of al-Andalus (of coexistence and mutual flourishing between outsiders and natives), even if he questions the reality of that dream, whether it existed "on earth . . . or in the poem" (still he asks us in "The 'Red Indian's' Penultimate Speech" whether we would "memorize a bit of poetry to halt the slaughter"). "Granada is my body," he sings, "Granada is my country. / And I come from there." The "descent" is not the "Arab" laying claim to distant lands and a glorious past—a clichéd annotation; it is the grand illumination against the "cleansing" of the other, in revenge or otherwise, in the past or the future, embodied in the "dream" of al-Andalus that could not save itself from the horrors of history.

While each of the eleven sections in "The Andalusian Scene" is a stand-alone poem, the entire sequence is a love poem that embraces time and place "in the departure to one essence" and touches the deep bond Darwish had with Federico García Lorca and his "bedouin moon." "The 'Red Indian's' Penultimate Speech" should also be read beyond the comparative impulse or historical allegory (Darwish composed the poem after listening repeatedly to Native American chants) and as a defense against the destruction of the earth, as a celebration of the earth: "Do not kill the grass anymore, the grass has a soul in us that defends / the soul in the earth." "Our names are trees of the deity's speech, and birds that soar higher / than the rifle," so "if our murder is imperative, then do not / kill the animals that have befriended us"; "do / you know the deer will not chew the grass if our blood touches it?"

"A Canaanite Rock in the Dead Sea" re-treats (into) the "father" and reaffirms "I am I" in an "absence entirely trees." The lyric begins with "my poem / is a rock flying to my father as a partridge does." In Arabic, "partridge" is also the word for "skip" or "hop"—exactly the rhythm of this poem. Ablation of myth is rewritten through the Canaanite "pigeon tower" and through the sharing of the earth. "We Will Choose Sophocles" switches to the collective in a discourse that weaves ancient and contemporary identity, a gentle living that has "the taste of small differences among the seasons," where "the mallow climbs the ancient shields / and its red flowers hide what the sword has done to the name."

Another significance of the poem stems from the mention of two literary characters placed in opposition: Imru' el-Qyss, prince of Kinda, the great pre-Islamic (Jahili) Arab poet, who sought Caesar's help (to avenge his father's murder) and failed and died as consequence of this option; and Sophocles, who rejected and mocked political authority and power. This coincides with the looming failure of the 1993 Oslo peace accords. Darwish's invocation of the Greek dramatist's lines—"He who makes the journey / To one in power is / His slave even if when / He set out he was free"—is haunting. His rejection of the peace façade is both firm and tender, a theme he develops in a 1996 poem, "A Non-linguistic Dispute with Imru' el-Qyss": "Our blood wasn't speaking in microphones on / that day, the day we leaned on a language that dispersed / its heart when it changed its path. No one / asked Imru' el-Qyss: What have you done / to us and to yourself? Go now on Caesar's / path, after a smoke that looks out through / time, black. Go on Caesar's path, alone, alone, alone, / and leave, right here, for us, your language!" And again later in *Mural*, with growing disinterest that highlights the mutability of recurrence or circularity in the Darwish poem: "I tired of what my language / on the backs of horses says or doesn't say / about the days of Imru' el-Qyss, / who was scattered between Caesar and rhyme."

The conundrum whereby the Palestinian tragedy is not permitted to "belong to the victim's question" "without interruption" clouds the reading of Darwish's poetry for many. "I am he, my self's coachman, / no horse whinnies in my language," Darwish would say in *Exile* in 2005, asserting his supreme concern with his art, independence, and individuality. Still, in "Rita's Winter," a love poem that returns us to Darwish's affair with dialogue, the private is at its most triumphant in these two collections. "Rita" is a pseudonym for Darwish's first love, a Jewish Israeli woman who became a cultural icon in the Arab world after the renowned Lebanese musician and singer Marcel Khalife sang one of Darwish's youthful poems, "Rita and the Rifle": "There's a rifle between Rita and me / and whoever knows Rita bows / and prays / to a god in those honey eyes . . ." "O Rita / nothing could turn your eyes away from mine / except a snooze / some honey clouds / and this rifle." The rifle connotes the Israeli military, in which Rita enlisted (and which perhaps reappears as the handgun placed on "the poem's draft" in the final lines of "Rita's Winter"). There were at least four more Rita poems in the 1960s and 70s. In "The Sleeping Garden" in 1977, for example, Darwish wrote: "Rita sleeps . . . sleeps then wakes her dreams: / Shall we get married? / Yes. / When? / When violet grows / on the soldier's helmet . . ." "I love you, Rita. I love you. Sleep / and I will ask you in thirteen winters: / Are you still sleeping?" Rita would sleep for fifteen additional winters before she would make her return in 1992, her final appearance in a Darwish poem.

———

As I said, *Mural*'s significance stems from a great artist's engagement with death in his late years: the simultaneity of art and mortality, the objective and the subjective, on two parallel lanes of what is left of time in a body or, as Theodor Adorno termed it, "the catastrophe" of "late style" (an ironic expression for a Palestinian). *Mural* begins a period of elusive abandon in Darwish's poetry, an ease with what language may bring. He puts it another way in "I Don't Know the Stranger," a poem from 2005: "The dead are equal before death, they don't speak / and probably don't dream . . . / and this stranger's funeral might have been mine / had it not been for a divine matter that postponed it / for many reasons, among them / an error in my poem." This righting of the poem's wrong life—this potential philosophic "error" (which also shadows the eleventh-century Arab poet-philosopher al-Ma'arri) upon which Darwish embarked—was a chronic concern for him. In *Mural*, certain elements of his youthful aesthetic, namely dialogue and more casual diction, return and are now redeemed by age. Pithy narrative stitches the lyric epic into drama on the stage. Monologue belongs to several voices. Darwish's dramatic theater (of "The Tragedy of Narcissus" or "The Hoopoe") incorporates several styles of dialogue and quotidian settings. For example, the terse, concise line-by-line chat between Darwish and his prison guard toward the poem's end is a continuation of the conversational tone that resurfaced in short lyrics in *Why Did You Leave the Horse Alone?* (1996), was mastered in *Don't Apologize for What You've Done* (2003), and became fully available in the lyric epic in *Exile* (2005).

Mural rotates setting and scene in three major movements between a hospital room, Death, and the poet's visions and conversations. The poem opens with the nurse and the poet's "horizontal" name, Darwish's awareness of his death, his ensuing search for meaning and existence. He becomes "the dialogue of dreamers," a bird, a vineyard, and a poet whose language is "a metaphor for metaphor." But the nurse swiftly returns and interrupts him in an important moment that heralds the full realization of the name in the final pages of *Mural* (when the "horizontal name" becomes vertical abecedary). For now, however, a woman nurse says: "This is your name, remember it well! / And don't disagree with it over a letter / or concern yourself with tribal banners, / be a friend to your horizontal name, / try it out on the dead and the living, teach it / accurate pronunciation in the company of strangers," "a stranger is another stranger's brother. / We will seize the feminine with a vowel promised to the flutes." Then Darwish is reunited with his first love, his first goddess and first legends, his stranger self, his "other" and "alternate."

Early in the poem Darwish (who was shy, generous, and modest) is quite aware of the unfolding play that has become his life, between perception and illusion, the private and the public, poem and being: "Am I he? / Do I perform my role well in the final act?" "or did the victim change / his affidavit to live the postmodern moment, / since the author strayed from the script / and the actors and spectators have gone?" Characters (including "Echo" and "Death") enter and exit the lyrical fantasy of the poet. He is "one who talks to himself" and one who "sang to weigh the spilled vastness / in the ache of a dove." And he arrives at an essential truth of his art: "my poem's land is green and high," a celebration of being alive, and of the earth, because "there is no nation smaller than its poem," and "the earth is the festival of losers" to whom Darwish belongs (perhaps as the absented poet of Troy). And he returns to his poem's features: "the narcissus contemplating the water of its image," "the clarity of shadows in synonyms," "the speech of prophets on the surface of night," "the donkey of wisdom . . . mocking the poem's reality and myth," "the congestion of symbol with its opposites," "the other 'I' / writing its diaries in the notebooks of lyricists . . . at the gates of exile," and "echo as it scrapes the sea salt / of [his] language off the walls." The nurse reenters, and the poet catalogs visions and dreams induced by sedatives: memories of his father's death, his mother's bread, his exile from his language and place, and his kinship to dead poets and philosophers. He realizes he is still alive, that his "hour hasn't arrived," and summons his favorite goddess, Anat, to sing since "life might come suddenly, / to those disinclined to meaning, from the wing of a butterfly / caught in a rhyme."

"And I want to live," he declares to begin the second and perhaps best-known movement of *Mural*. This vivid and occasionally humorous dialogue with Death is timeless writing. Darwish is neither waiting for Godot nor bargaining with Faustus. He leaves us his will (which he knows will not be followed when he dies), perhaps to authenticate the separateness of his private self from what the larger collective perceives it to be (though in death, the gap becomes narrow): "Death! wait for me, until I finish / the funeral arrangements in this fragile spring, / when I was born, when I would prevent the sermonizers / from repeating what they said about the sad country / and the resistance of olives and figs in the face / of time and its army. I will tell them: Pour me / in the *Nūn*, where my soul gulps / Surat al-Rahman in the Quran," and "Don't put violets on my grave: violets are / for the depressed, to remind the dead of love's / premature death. Put seven green ears / of wheat on the coffin instead, and some / anemones, if either can be found. Otherwise, leave the roses / of the church to the church and the weddings. / Death, wait, until I pack my suitcase: / my toothbrush, my soap, / my electric razor, cologne, and clothes. / Is the climate temperate there? / Do conditions change in the eternal whiteness / or do they remain the same in autumn / as in winter? Is one book enough / to entertain me in timelessness, or will I need / a library? And what's the spoken language there: / colloquial for all, or classical Arabic?"

With irony and resolve, Darwish embraces and humanizes the self and others, where he is simultaneously a lyrical letter in the Quran and "at ease with the Old Testament's narrative" as the beautiful Joseph, whose vision is of abundance and fertility in "seven green ears / of wheat." Even Arabic is an "I" indivisible from its "other," an "exterior" within an "interior." And as Darwish goes on in this wonderful dialogue with Death, paradox and parody ("Death, wait, have a seat," "perhaps / the star wars have tired you today?") grow into exultation ("all the arts have defeated you") and provocation ("you are the only exile, poor you," "How do you walk like this without guards or a singing choir, / like a coward thief"). But this frivolity does not last long, and the poet comes clean with Death because the two of them "on God's road / are two Sufis who are governed by vision / but don't see." Still, Darwish insists, despite Death's indifference, on meeting by the sea gate, where the poem will eventually close, in Akko, the port of his childhood, seven kilometers from his razed village, al-Birweh, in Galilee. And as with the hospital scene and the name, "this sea" will eventually become present to announce the poem's end.

The third movement begins as the nurse reappears and "the death of language" has passed. In one of the poem's more memorable stanzas, in a recurring scene between patient and nurse, she says to him: "You used to hallucinate / often and scream at me: / I don't want to return to anyone, / I don't want to return to any country / after this long absence . . . / I only want to return / to my language in the distances of cooing." In this extreme moment of personality disconcerted with geographical "return," in the artist's tremendous and volatile gripping of his medium, "the distances of cooing," their quietude and serene imagination paradoxically affirm "return" to a region beyond the political or historical, therefore more lasting, more durable. The poem remains "green and high," and the poet writes it down "patiently, to the meter / of seagulls in the book of water," and "to the scattering / of wheat ears in the book of the field." Again he praises: "I am the grain / of wheat that has died to become green again. / And in my death there is a kind of life . . ." And as is Darwish's custom of uniting art with life, he tells us of what he has fathered: "I preferred the free marriage between words . . . / the feminine will find the suitable masculine / in poetry's leaning toward prose . . ." Between "the sentimental" and "thousands of romantic years" the poet carves "a tattoo in identity" where "The personal is not personal. / The universal not universal . . ."

Darwish returns to myth, the mirror image of the poem's first movement, a circular aesthetic. Anat, the Sumerian and Canaanite goddess, reappears, scriptures persist, but new characters and subjects also appear: Gilgamesh, Enkidu, Osiris, King Solomon, and the Book of Ecclesiastes. He meets his boy self, his girl love, his prison guard, and his childhood horse. With each encounter Darwish rewrites anew what he had written in the past (as in the story of his imprisonment) or what he would rewrite in the future (as in the horse that guided his family back to an unconscious boy Darwish who fell off it one wild night when he took it out for a ride). Perhaps "the horse" exemplifies the excessive reading that frequently goes into Darwish's "symbols," whereas in fact these "symbols" are often private memories. Perhaps it is the same horse who saved Darwish's life that the poet addresses toward the end of *Mural*: "Persist, my horse, we no longer differ in the wind . . . / you're my youth and I'm your imagination. Straighten / like an *Aleph*," "You're my pretext, and I'm your metaphor / away from riders who are tamed like destinies." Perhaps it is an appeal to that elemental bond that granted him life once that it might grant it again, in a delightful dance between the pastoral and the postmodern: "Don't die before me, horse, or after me, or with me / on the final slope. And look inside the ambulances, / stare at the dead . . . I might still be living."

The plethora of actors and dialogue accelerates and gathers suspense in a radiance that lends itself to the imagination on the stage. And in preparation for the finale, Darwish announces that "as Christ walked on the lake, / I walked in my vision. But I came down / from the cross because I have a fear of heights and don't / promise Resurrection. I only changed / my cadence to hear my heart clearly." This declaration of his fragility goes on to speak the most delicate assertion of his po-

etry: "The epicists have falcons, and I have / *The Collar of the Dove*," the wings of
love that would return him to Akko's port, as he had mentioned in an earlier poem,
"Ivory Combs," where his "mother had lost her handkerchiefs"; or maybe it is as
he retells it in *Mural*: "I might / add the description of Akko to the story / the old-
est beautiful city / the loveliest old city / a stone box / where the dead and the
living move / in its clay as if in a captive beehive." Darwish begins the final ascen-
sion of *Mural* and recounts what is his, starting with Akko's sea, his semen, and
down to the two meters of this earth that would house his 175-centimeter horizon-
tal body, and his return to his horizontal name, now loosened into vertical lines
whose alliterative luminosity will remain the privacy of his language, the lan-
guage of the *Dhād*, impossible to translate otherwise. And the simply complex no-
tion of his existence, and of anyone's being, becomes an eternal calling: "I am not
mine / I am not mine / I am not mine."

━━━

Five years and three books after *Mural*, in 2005, Darwish was still writing, still
searching for the self within its others, through new lyric form. *Exile* is a play in
verse that "neither linger[s] . . . nor hurr[ies]" in a mature prosody like "life's sim-
ple prose," even if intransigently lyrical and giddy in parts. *Exile* has its "bridge"
and could simply be "the cunning of eloquence" or "the backdrop of the epic
scene." And "return" is "a comedy by one of our frivolous goddesses." If dialogue
or dialectic and its supporting cast were spontaneous and major expressions in the
totality of Darwish's language in *Mural*, they became a more purposeful aesthetic
of the theater of the lyric epic in *Exile*: four quartets, each with a setting and at
least two characters, palpable or spectral, named or unnamed (of which the "I" is
constant among them); choral modes or interludes are regularly introduced (es-
pecially in the first three movements); memory and vision stand in for scenes

within each act; the entire sequence is a dialogue that alternates between the absurd and the expository. *Exile* walks in strata or polyphony: of love and pleasure ("If the canary doesn't sing /to you, my friend"); of place ("What is place?" "The senses' discovery of a foothold /for intuition"); of time (where one and his ghost "fly, as a Sufi does, in the words . . . to anywhere"); and of art (where "aesthetic is only the presence /of the real in form," "a freedom" that bids "farewell to the poem /of pain").

The first quartet finds the poet strolling on a Tuesday when "the weather is clear" "as if [he] were another." After remembrance and forgetting, and wonderful discursiveness, he meets his lover. ("My lexicon is Sufi. My desires are sensory / and I am not who I am /unless the two meet: /I and the feminine I," he would write in *The Dice Player* in 2008.) Unlike Rita, the "feminine" in "Tuesday and the Weather Is Clear" is not named, yet the personal detail is equally intimate, if not more so. And as the two part, the poet continues to walk until he finds himself in the throes of his private language and conducts a brilliant appeal to it, almost a prayer: "O my language, /help me to adapt and embrace the universe"; "My language, will I become what you'll become, or are you /what becomes of me? Teach me the wedding parade /that merges the alphabet with my body parts. / Teach me to become a master not an echo"; "For who, if I utter what isn't poetry, /will understand me? Who will speak to me of a hidden / longing for a lost time if I utter what isn't poetry? /And who will know the stranger's land?. . ."

In the second sequence, the self moves into its masculine other "on the bridge," where fog competes with vision at dawn. A dialectic, where "a thing cannot be known by its opposite," dominates "Dense Fog over the Bridge," which pushes the limits of obsession and rumination until it delivers perhaps the last intense lyric spell in Darwish's poetry, a dream approaching "fever" in sixteen successive quatrains that speak of jasmine and "every -ology" until the "I" reaches "the land of story." "Dense Fog" certainly invokes the Jericho Bridge (formerly the Allenby Bridge, after the British general who conquered Jerusalem in 1917). The bridge has become iconic for Palestinians and continues to serve as an oppressive checkpoint for those crossing between Jordan and the West Bank. It was on this bridge, for example, that Darwish was recently interrogated and asked, as the famous poet, to recite some of his poems, to which he replied: "A prisoner does not sing to his prison warden."

Darwish managed to transform this subjugation into a more profound dialogue in his poetry, where the physicality of the bridge, and of those on it, is and is not itself. (Like "river," the manifestation of "bridge" in Darwish's late poetry is worthy of independent study. See, for example, "We Walk on the Bridge," or the occurrence of "river" in poems like "A Cloud from Sodom" or "A Mask ... for Majnoon Laila.") Recurrence simply seeks "the thing itself," or, as he said in "The Southerner's House" in 2003, "the transparency of the thing." And the journey home becomes more beautiful than home: "On the bridge," the mystery that was "extreme clarity" in "The Tragedy of Narcissus" becomes "neither mysterious nor clear," "like a dawn that yawns a lot." And Jericho (which was one of the first cities handed over to "Palestinian control" under the "peace agreement") is simply exposed: "Don't promise me anything / don't give me / a rose from Jericho." Darwish was looking "not for a burial place" but "a place to live in, to curse" if he wished it so. Short of that, he would continue to rotate on "the bridge," between entry and exit, interior and exterior, "like a sunflower," while absence is still "wearing trees." And he would be content with the "work [he has left] to do in myth."

And walking farther, toward this new task in myth, Darwish stumbles onto his ghost, his shadow, the archetypal exile, the wandering human, personified in the pre-Islamic Arab poet Tarafah Ibn al-Abd (who is also mentioned in *Mural*, and paired with "existentialists"). The title of the poem, "Like a Hand Tattoo in the

Jahili Poet's Ode," draws from the opening line of Tarafah's famous ode, which describes the ruins of the beloved's dwelling that "sway like the remnants of a tattoo on the back of a hand." The poem is suspended between two shadows of the same self, one that urges the other to "drop metaphor, and take a stroll on the woolly earth," while the other is deceived by "a cloud [that] knits its identity around [him]." This paradox is held in balance between "two epochs": the first "imagination's return to the real," the relics of "an ancestral notion," and the second "a butterfly trace in the light." (Thus "Hand Tattoo" is significant as an *ars poetica* that combines two major aesthetics of the history of Arab poetics in one poem.)

Darwish's easing of the lyric intensity takes hold in "Hand Tattoo" (and prepares the reader for "Counterpoint," the final quartet). The poem addresses the marginalized account of the Palestinian narrative in more personal and informal speech. "And as for anthem, the anthem of happy finale / has no poet." A third voice is eventually introduced. It grounds dialogue between the two, like "a bulldozer / driver who changed the spontaneity of this place / and cut the braids of your olive trees to match / the soldiers' hair." Governed by silence and absence, pointed dialogue follows. The struggle to break free from the shackles of identity in "Hand Tattoo" remains as it was in "The Hoopoe": "Place is the passion." And flight "in the words . . . to anywhere" also persists. Still the "I and I" seek to "make amends" with their relics, since "in the presence of death we grasp only the accuracy of our names," a quotidian existentiality that is sieved through the mystery of identity. However, in time, "I and I" "found not one stone / that carries a victim's name," "a lewd absurdity."

Darwish does not resolve the poem and takes myth into the satiric final lines, which expose the eroticization of a place and its people, no matter how language subverts the plot of power. If Darwish had previously attempted to upend myth and history, through the affirmation of the ancient (Canaanite) self, and through fraternity with a larger human narrative, he now comes full circle to the "lewd absurdity" that turns a victim into a new fascination of a "foreign tourist who loves [the native's] myths" and would love "to marry one of [his goddess's] widowed daughters." It's a startling ending of a very serious poem, a determined "frivolous" conclusion, in fact, and it returns us to the poem's beginning, when the poet wished his name had "fewer letters, / easier letters on the foreign woman's ears," a spoof and an almost elegiac reverberation of the nurse's instruction to Darwish regarding his name at the beginning of *Mural*.

This amusement and irreconcilability, this "late style," is a highly developed form of aesthetic resistance ("Every beautiful poem is an act of resistance," Darwish later wrote). It is fitting, therefore, that in the final movement of *Exile*, Edward Said appears, side by side with Darwish, where, on the one hand, "the intellectual reins in the novelist's rendition," and on the other, "the philosopher dissects the singer's rose." The two protagonists converge and part over exile as "two in one / like a sparrow's wings," in diction that seems like talk over coffee or dinner. Identity is exposed as "self-defense" that should not be "an inheritance / of a past" but is what its "owner creates": "I am the plural. Within my interior / my renewing exterior resides." And Darwish's final lines, his "farewell to the poem / of pain," embrace "the impossible" and "the suitable," "words / that immortalize their readers," one of the legacies he leaves behind and entrusts to us.

———

For the longest time I have been drawn to a passage on "intention" in Theodor Adorno's *Minima Moralia*. He talks about film, image, and reproduction, but the passage also brings to mind the "use" or "function" of poetry: "True intentions would only be possible by renouncing intention," Adorno says, and this "stems from the [ambiguous] concept of significance." Significance hits the mark when "the objective figure, the realized expression, turns outward from itself and speaks"; equally, significance goes astray when "the figure is corrupted by counting in the interlocutor." This "danger" must be undertaken in a work of art: "Significant form, however esoteric, makes concessions to consumption; lack of significance is dilettantism by its immanent criteria. Quality is decided by the depth at which the work incorporates the alternatives within itself, and so masters them."

This seems to me a profound account of Darwish's work. Intention in his poetry gives way to language, in lyric form, without ever losing significance, despite the hazardous paradox of public appropriation of the work, which Darwish always guarded against by engaging several other selves; a spherical form, or an "orbit I never lose," as he said in "Hand Tattoo." "There is no love that is not an echo," Adorno says in another entry, and so it is for Darwish. Echo is return. Echo is reciprocity, and also the distance necessary for the "I" to reach its "other," for the "other" to recognize its "I." At a book signing for *Like Almond Blossoms or Farther* in Ramallah, 2005, Darwish wrote: "The Palestinian is not a profession or a slogan. He, in the first place, is a human being who loves life and is taken by almond blossoms and feels a shiver after the first autumn rain," "and this means the long occupation has failed to erase our human nature, and has not succeeded in submitting our language and emotions to the drought desired for them at the checkpoint." "Words are not land or exile" but the "density of a stanza that isn't written with letters" and "the yearning to describe the whiteness of almond blossoms."

Darwish would not neglect "the poem's end," he would leave "the door open / for the Andalus of lyricists, and [choose] to stand / on the almond and pomegranate fence, shaking / the spiderwebs off [his] grandfather's aba / while a foreign army was marching / the same old roads, measuring time / with the same old war machine." He clearly merges East and West (where "the East is not completely East /

and the West is not completely West"), and the repetitive processing and expansion of lexicon and memory stand for a philosophy. The list of great writers who inform his poetry (or coincide with it, and he with theirs) is not merely a reflection of influence but an assertion of the shared well of human knowledge and spirit. "A poet is made up of a thousand poets," he used to say. He became deeply enmeshed in the complex, rich history of Arabic literary thought as he wrote a language for his time. His treatment of dialectic, metaphysics, mysticism, recurrence, form, and duality, among other things, deserves more advanced study than I can offer, but it also demands a daring, unapologetic openness to life, humanity, and the world: "If I were another I would have belonged to the road"; "become two / on this road: I . . . and another"; "If I were another I would leave this white paper and converse with a Japanese novel whose author climbs to the mountaintop to see what predator and marauder birds have done with his ancestors. Perhaps he is still writing, and his dead are still dying. But I lack the experience, and the metaphysical harshness"; "if I were another / I might still be myself the second time around."

SOURCES

Adonis, *Sufism and Surrealism* (Saqi Books, 2005).

Theodor Adorno, *Minima Moralia* (Verso, 1974).

Sinan Antoon, "Mahmud Darwish's Allegorical Critique of Oslo," *Journal of Palestine Studies* 31, no. 2 (Winter 2002).

Mahmoud Darwish, *The Butterfly's Burden* (Copper Canyon Press, 2007).

Reginald Gibbons, "Sophokles the Poet," *American Poetry Review* 37, no. 6 (November/December 2008).

Georg Lukács, *The Historical Novel* (Merlin Press, 1989).

Edward W. Said, *On Late Style: Music and Literature Against the Grain* (Vintage, 2008).

I SEE WHAT I WANT

1990

... As I look behind me in this night
into the tree leaves and the leaves of life
as I stare into the water's memory and the memory of sand
I do not see in this night
other than the end of this night
the ticking clock gnaws at my life by the second
and shortens the life of this night
nothing of the night or of me remains to wrestle over ... or about
but the night goes back to its night
and I fall into this shadow's pit

RUBAIYAT

1.

I see what I want of the field . . . I see
braids of wheat combed by the wind, and I close my eyes:
this mirage leads to a nahawand
and this serenity to lapis

2.

I see what I want of the sea . . . I see
the rise of seagulls at sunset, and I close my eyes:
this loss leads to an Andalus
and this sail is the pigeons' prayer for me . . .

3.

I see what I want of the night . . . I see
the end of this long corridor by some city's gates.
I'll toss my notebook on the sidewalk of cafés, and seat this absence
on a chair aboard one of the ships

4.

I see what I want of the soul: the face of stone
as lightning scratches it. Green is the land ... green, the land of my soul.
Wasn't I a child once playing by the edge of the well?
I am still playing ... this vastness is my meadow, and the stones my wind

5.

I see what I want of peace ... I see
a gazelle, grass, and a rivulet ... I close my eyes:
This gazelle sleeps on my arms
and its hunter sleeps near the gazelle's children in a distant place

6.

I see what I want of war ... I see
our ancestors' limbs squeeze the springs green in a stone,
and our fathers inherit the water but bequeath nothing. So I close my eyes:
The country within my hands is of my hands

7.

I see what I want of prison: a flower's days
passed through here to guide two strangers within me
to a bench in the garden, then I close my eyes:
Spacious is the land, beautiful through a needle's eye

8.

I see what I want of lightning . . . I see
the vegetation of the fields crumble the shackles, O joy!
Joy for the white almond song descending on the smoke of villages
like doves . . . What we feed our children we share with the doves

9.

I see what I want of love . . . I see
horses making the meadow dance, fifty guitars sighing, and a swarm
of bees suckling the wild berries, and I close my eyes
until I see our shadow behind this dispossessed place

10.

I see what I want of death: I love, and my chest splits
for a horse of Eros that leaps out of it white, running over clouds
and flying on endless vapor, circling the eternal blue . . .
So do not stop me from dying, do not bring me back to a star of dust

11.

I see what I want of blood: I have seen the murdered
address the murderer who bullet-lit his heart: From now on
you shall remember only me. I, too, murdered you idly, and from now on
you shall remember only me . . . you won't bear the roses of spring

12.

I see what I want of the theater of the absurd: beasts,
court judges, the emperor's hat, the masks of the era,
the color of the ancient sky, the palace dancer, the mayhem of armies.
Then I forget them all and remember only the victim behind the curtain

13.

I see what I want of poetry: in ancient times, we used to parade martyred
poets in sweet basil then return to their poetry safely. But in this age
of humming, movies, and magazines, we heap the sand on their poems
and laugh. And when we return we find them standing at our doorsteps . . .

14.

I see what I want of dawn in the dawn . . . I see
nations looking for their bread in other nations' bread. It is bread
that ravels us from the silk of sleepiness, and from the cotton of our dreams.
So is it from a grain of wheat that the dawn of life bursts . . . and also the
    dawn of war?

15.

I see what I want of people: their desire to long
for anything, their lateness in getting to work,
and their hurry to return to their folk . . .
and their need to say: Good Morning . . .

TAKE CARE OF THE STAGS, FATHER

... Resigned to your father's steps I went looking for you, Father, there
at the burning of my fingers with the candles of your thorns, when
the sunset pruned the carob tree, and when we—your father and I—
were behind you as your parents.
You were hanging from your hands on the cactus in the plains
and our fears for you, like an eagle, hovered above you.
You must bequeath the sky from the sky.
You must bear a land like the skin of the soul punctured by chicory blossoms.
You must choose your ax out of their rifles that are upon you.
You must be partial, Father, to the profit of dew in your palms
and to your abandoned wheat around the military camps,
do as you please with your jailers' hearts, and resist despite the thorns,
when the neighing conquers you from the six directions, resist,
for the plains, the plains are yours.

... And my father is shy, Father, what does he say ... that you don't.
I spoke with him about himself but he gestured to the winter, hid something
in the ashes. Don't give me love, I whispered, I want to give the land
a gazelle instead. Explain your distant beginning for me, Father, to see you as I do,
a teacher of the book of earth, from *Aleph* to *Ya'*, and plant me there.
Birth is a riddle, Father: it sprouts like oak and splits the rock within
the threshold of this naked scene then ascends ... then blackness breaks it.

We crawl then we're adolescent. The mares rise and gallop into vastness.
We tumble then we're quiescent. When were we born, Father, and when
will we die? But he, the shy one, doesn't reply, and time is in his hands, he sends it
to the wadi and brings it back, he's the garden in its simple stature.
He doesn't speak to me of the history of his days:
We were here before time and we shall remain here for the fields to become green.
Take care of the stags . . . nurture them in the large courtyard of the house, Father!
But he turns his gaze away from me. Mends a grapevine. Offers
some wheat and water to the horse. Greets him slowly, cajoles him and whispers:
You're the purebred. He takes the mint my mother hands him. Smokes
his tobacco. Tallies the grape chandeliers and says to me: Settle down!
Then I doze on his knee on the numbness of fatigue . . .

I recall the plants: the chrysanthemum flock leads me to Aleppo.
My imagination takes me past the mountain of the flute, I run after the flute
and run after the birds to learn to fly. I have hidden my secret
in what the forefathers say, there behind the hill. You have often distanced me
from what I try to be and not be . . . you know
I want what the flowers give, not the salt. You have often brought me near
the distant star of futility, Father. Why didn't you for once in your life
call me: Son! . . . so I would fly to you after school? Why didn't you try to raise me
as you raised your field into sesame, corn, and wheat? Is it because
what's in you of wars is a soldier's dread of the chrysanthemum in the houses?
Be my master so I may flee you to the shepherds on the hills.
Be my master for my mother to love me . . .
for my brothers to forget the banana crescent.
Be my master that I may memorize more of the Quran . . . love the feminine

and become her master and imprison her with me!

Be my master that I may see the guide.

You hid your heart from me, Father, so I'd grow up suddenly alone in the palm trees.

Trees, ideas, and a mizmar . . . I will leap from your hands to departure

and march against the wind, against our sunset . . . My exile is a land.

A land of desires, Canaanite, herding the stags and mountain goats . . .

A land of words the pigeons carry to the pigeons . . . and you're an exile.

An exile of incursions speech delivers to speech . . . you're a land

of mint under my poems, drawing near and going far

in a conqueror's name, then again in a new conqueror's name, a ball

snatched by invaders and fixed above the ruins of temples and above the soldiers.

Ancient son of Canaan! if you were made of stone

the weather would have been different.

But they wrote their anthem over you, for you to become "he-you" the lonely.

No lily ever came to witness who was her martyr poet.

The historian stole my language and my lily, Father, and banished me

from the divine promise. And when I faced him with my ancestors'

bones, he cried: "My Lord . . . my Lord

why didn't they all die so you would become mine alone . . . ?"

A cactus punctured your heart, Father. Do you forgive what I did with your heart

when I grew up alone, when I went alone to look upon the poem from afar?

Why do you rush now toward the great journey when you're the Torah of the roots?

You have filled the jars with the first of the sacred oil, and fashioned a vineyard

out of rock. You endlessly said: Do not leave for Sidon or Tyre.

I am coming, this instant, Father, dead or alive! . . . Will you forgive my madness

with the birds of my questions about meaning? Will you forgive my longing

in this winter for a lavish suicide? I watched my heart and lost yours,
you had hidden it from me for too long, then I resorted to the moon.
Say: I love you . . . before you doze, and before the rain comes tumbling down.

. . . Enmeshed in brown wool, leaning on the tree's steps
he gazes into his missing paradise, behind his hands, casts his shadow
over the dirt, his dirt, then pulls it . . . he catches a chrysanthemum
with his aba's shadow, but cannot fool the thief of trees.
Is this my father who flings his arrows of shadow toward his stolen
dirt to snatch a chrysanthemum from it . . . before nightfall?
How many new armies will occupy time?
They come to war within themselves in us, these princes, and we're the martyrs.
They come, build citadels upon citadels, then go, and we remain who we are.
This beast steals our skin and sleeps in it on our bedsheets, this beast
bites us then wails from the ache of longing for the eyes of chrysanthemum.
Land! why am I your strange visitor on the spears of those who come from smoke?
Land, I've never asked you whether the place has already left the place behind.
There is one meter between my blond fields and me . . .
a scissor-meter that cuts my heart.
I am from here . . . I saw my guts looking upon me through the corn fuzz.
I saw my memory counting the seeds of this field and the martyrs within it.
I am from here. I am right here . . . I comb the olives in this autumn.
I am from here. And here I am. That's what my father shouted: I am from here.
And here I am. I am I. And here is here. I am I. And I am here. Here
I am. And I am I. Here I am. I am here. And here I am. I am I . . .
Then echo approached. Broke the vastness. Its resurrection rose. An echo

finding an echo. And echo resounded: Forever here forever here . . .
Then time became tomorrow, and the shape of echo appeared as a country,
and sent death back. So break the wall of the universe, Father, as an echo
surrounding echo; and explode:
I am
from
here
and here
is here
and I
am I
and here
I am
and I
am here.

The earth cracks its eggshell and swims between us
green beneath the clouds. The sky of color adorns her
and bewitches us, she the blue the green, born out of her legend,
out of the sacrificial feast of her wheat. She teaches us the art of searching
for the myth of creation, a woman upon her water arcades,
a woman ruling the eulogies. Age doesn't blemish her face. A bull
doesn't carry her on his horns. She carries herself within herself and sleeps
in the lap of herself. She doesn't bid us farewell or greet strangers.
And doesn't remember the past. She has no past.
She's herself, to and for herself. She lives and we live

when she lives free and green. She didn't board a single train with us. Not a camel
or a plane. And didn't lose any of her offspring. Didn't move far from us and didn't
lose her minerals. She didn't lose her allure. She's the green upon her blue waters . . .
   So rise, Father, from among the temple ruins and write
   your name on her ring as the forefathers had written their names.
   Rise to love your beautiful wife, from her braids to her anklets.
   Rise! The only olive in this land's olive is the shadow of the land,
   so rise to praise it, to worship it, and tell the tale of forgetfulness:
The invaders have often passed through and changed you and changed the names
of the land, repaired their vehicles and shared the martyrs of the land,
the land that remained what it used to be, your woman and your mother.
So rise, Father, let singing bring you back
like anemones that adopt the land and sing her as a house for the sky.

. . . And why the poem, Father? Winter is winter.
I will sleep after you, after this fragile carnival where the blood blackens
on the statues of temples like wine . . . where narcissus and water break the lovers
who break their jealousy, their rift, and the crystal of longing for longing.
And I am sad, Father, like a pigeon in a tower, removed from its flock.
I am sad, Father, so if you meet my grandfather bid him salaam.
Kiss his hands, for me and for the descendants of Baal and Anat.
And fill his jug with wine from the grapes of Galilee or Hebron, and tell him:
My woman refuses to be the frame of her image. She exits from my remains
like another phoenix. And if you meet me there, Father, also bid me salaam.
Forget that I overlooked your horses, forgive, so I may know my memories.
You had hidden your heart from me, Father, before my life sheltered me within
what I see of creatures that don't make me . . . But now

your remote fatherhood pulls at my hands and at my scattering

by your shadow's window, pulls toward the adobe shadow that hangs in the poem . . .

Birth is a riddle . . . I asked you, Father: Were you born to die?

You have often set your life aside . . . exhausted yourself . . . promised

to live for tomorrow but never lived at all. What good is the poem?

It raises the ceiling of our caves and flies from our blood to the language of doves.

O master of shrouded trees over the shadow of lavender's shadow,

master of the stone whose blood your palms wrung out . . . have you exited

the marble to return to it? Tell me why did you bring me here, Father . . . why?

Is it so I can call out when I'm tired: O Father, my friend?

O friend! Which one of us died before the other . . .

     I?

     Or my friend?

TRUCE WITH THE MONGOLS

BY THE HOLM OAK FOREST

Some creatures of holm oak have been standing long there on the hill . . . perhaps
the grass will rise from our bread toward them if we leave the place, and perhaps
the heavenly lapis will descend from them toward the shadow over the citadels.
But who will fill up our ceramics after us? Who will alter our enemies when
they know we are climbing the hill to praise God . . .

> in creatures of holm oak?

Everything points to the absurdity of the wind, yet we don't rise in vain.
Maybe this morning is not as heavy upon us as yesterday, we have
prolonged our stay before the sky and worshipped only what we have lost
of our worship. Maybe the earth is more spacious than its description. Maybe
this road is a way in with the wind . . .

> to the forest of holm oak

The victims march on either side, say some final words, then fall into
one world. Yet the eagle and the holm oak will conquer them. There must be
a truce, then, for the anemones in the plains to conceal the dead, and for us
to exchange some curses before we reach the hill. There must be
a human fatigue that changes those horses . . .

> into creatures of holm oak

In the prairie, echo is one: an echo. And the sky on a stone
is an estrangement the birds hang up on this endless space, then fly . . .
And during the long wars, echo is one: a mother, a father, and a son
believed the horses behind the lakes will return tasseled with their final wish.
They brewed some coffee for their dreams to push away sleep . . .

                          amid the ghosts of holm oak

Each war teaches us to love nature more: after the siege
we care more for irises. We pick tenderness from almond trees
in March. We plant gardenias in marble and water our neighbors' plants
when they're out to hunt the gazelles. When will war set down its load
so we can loosen the waists of the women on the hill free . . .

                          of the knot of symbols in the holm oak?

If only our enemies would take our seats in myth, they'd learn
how much we love the pavement they detest . . . if they would take
the copper and lightning that are ours . . . we would take their silken boredom.
If only our enemies would read our letters twice or three times . . . and apologize
to the butterfly for their game of fire . . .

                          in the forest of holm oak

We have often desired peace for our lord in the heights . . . our lord in the books.
We have often desired peace for the wool weaver . . . for the child by the cavern
and for the lovers of life . . . for our enemies' children in their shelters . . .
for the Mongols when they would retire to nights filled with their wives, when
they would leave the buds of our flowers . . . and leave us

                          and the leaves of holm oak

Wars teach us to taste the air and praise the water. How many
nights must we rejoice with chestnuts and dried chickpeas in our pockets?
Or shall we forget our talent in absorbing drizzle and ask: Were
those who died capable of not dying, capable of beginning their narrative here?
Perhaps . . . perhaps we are able to praise wine and raise a glass

                                          to the widow of holm oak

Each heart that doesn't respond to the flute here falls into
the spider trap. Be patient, be patient and you will hear echo's reverberation
over the enemy's horses, because the Mongols love our wine
and want to wear the skin of our wives at night, they want to take
the poets of the tribe prisoner

                                          and cut down the holm oak

The Mongols want us to be as they want us to be,
a fistful of dust blowing to China or Persia. And they want us
to love all their songs so that the peace they want can take hold . . .
We will memorize their parables . . . we will forgive their deeds when they go
along with this evening to the wind of their fathers

                                          past the song of holm oak

They did not come to win. The legend is not their legend. They descend
from the departure of horses to Asia's ailing west, and they don't know
that we would resist Ghazan-Arghun for a thousand years.
The legend is not his. Soon he will enter
the religion of his murdered to learn the speech of Quraish . . .

                                          and the miracle of holm oak

Echo is one in the nights. And at night's crest we tally
the stars on our lord's chest, count the ages of our children, older by the year,
and the family goats under the clouds, and the Mongol dead, and our dead.
Echo is one in the nights: we will return one day, there must be
a Persian poet for this longing . . .

> for the language of holm oak

Wars teach us to love detail: the shape of our door keys,
how to comb our wheat with eyelashes and walk lightly on our land,
how to cherish the hours before sunset over the zanzalakht . . .
And wars teach us to see God's image in everything, and to bear
the burden of myths and take the beast out

> of the story of holm oak

We will have a hearty laugh with the worms in our bread, and the worms
in the waters of war. We will hang up our black flags, if we win, on the laundry line
then knit them into socks . . . and as for song, it must be raised
in the funerals of our immortal heroes . . . and as for women slaves
of war, they must be freed, and there must be a rain

> over the memory of holm oak

Beyond this evening we see what remains of the night. Soon
the free moon will drink the warrior's tea under the trees.
One moon for all, for both sides of the trench, for us and them,
but do they have behind these mountains mud houses, tea, and a flute?
Do they have basil, like ours, to call back those who are heading toward death . . .

> in the forest of holm oak?

... At last, we have climbed the hill. Here we are now rising

above the trunks of the story . . . new grass sprouts over our blood and theirs.

We will load our rifles with sweet basil and collar the necks of doves

with medals for those who have returned . . . so far

we have found no one to accept peace . . . we are not who we are

nor are the others themselves. The rifles are broken . . . and the doves fly far too far.

We found no one here . . .

we found no one . . .

we didn't find the forest of holm oak!

A MUSIC SENTENCE

A poet now, instead of me,
writes a poem
on the willow of distant wind.
So why does a rose in the wall
wear new petals?

A boy now, instead of us,
sets a dove flying
high toward the cloud ceiling.
So why does the forest shed all
this snow around a smile?

A bird now, instead of us,
carries a letter
from the land of the gazelle to the blue.
So why does the hunter enter the scene
and fling his arrow?

A man now, instead of us,
washes the moon
and walks over the river's crystal.
So why does color fall on the earth
and we are naked like trees?

A lover now, instead of me,
sweeps his love
into the mire of bottomless springs.
So why does the cypress stand here
like a watchman at the garden gate?

A horseman now, instead of me,
stops his horse
and dozes under the shadow of a holm oak.
So why do the dead flock
to us out of wall and closet?

THE TRAGEDY OF NARCISSUS

THE COMEDY OF SILVER

They returned . . .
from the end of the long tunnel to their mirrors . . . they returned
when they recovered their brothers' salt, single or in groups, they returned
from the myths of defending citadels to what is simple in speech.
They won't need to raise their hands or banners to miracles anymore, if they choose.
They returned to celebrate the water of their existence, to organize this air
and wed their sons to their daughters; to make a body hidden in marble dance
and to hang from their ceilings onions, okra, and garlic for winter,
to milk their goats and the clouds that flow from the pigeons' feathers.
They returned on the tips of their obsession to the geography of divine magic
and to the banana leaf mat in the land of ancient topography:
a mountain upon a sea;
     two lakes behind the memories,
        a coast for the prophets—
and a street for the scent of lemon. No harm befell the land.
The horse winds blew, the Hyksos blew, and the Tatars blew, masked
or unveiled. All immortalized their names with spear or mangonel . . . and departed.
None of them deprived April of its habits: the flowering out of stones
or the bells of lemon blossoms; no harm befell the sand—
no harm, not a harm after they left. And land, like language, is inherited.
The horse winds blew in and blew out, and the wheat burst from the wheat.

It was their choice to return and recover the fire in their flute,
so the far came from afar, bloodied with their clothes
and the fragile crystal, and the anthem rose —
above distance and absence. What kind of weapon impedes the soul
from its soaring? In each of their exiles there's a land that wasn't harmed . . .
They made their myth as they wished and pitched for the pebbles
the radiance of birds. And whenever they passed a river . . . they tore it,
burned it with longing . . . whenever they passed a lily
they cried and wondered: Are we a people or a wine for the new altar?

> Anthem! Take all the elements
> and take us higher
> slope by slope
> then descend to the valleys —
> Come anthem
> you know the place better
> you know the time better
> and how strong the things within us are . . .

They never went and never arrived; their hearts are almond seeds in the
streets. The plazas were more spacious than a sky that couldn't cover them. The
sea used to forget them. And they used to know their north and south, send the pi-
geons of memory to their first towers, and hunt, out of their martyrs, stars that
march them to the beast of childhood. Whenever they said: We arrived . . . the first
of them fell at the arch of beginning: O hero, stay far from us so we can walk in
you toward another ending, the beginning is damned. Hero, bloodied with long
beginnings, tell us: how many times will our journey be the beginning? Shrouded

hero, above wheat bread and almond wool, we will mummify the wound that ab-
sorbs your soul: with dew; with a sleepless night's milk; with the lemon blossom
and the bloodied stone; with anthem—our anthem; with a feather plucked from
the phoenix—

And land, like language, is inherited!

Their anthem is a stone scratching the sun.
They were kind and full of satire and didn't know dancing or the mizmar
except in the funerals of immigrant friends.
They used to love women the way they loved fruit and cats and principles.
They used to count the years by the ages of their dead, and migrate
to their obsessions: What did we do with the carnation to become its distance?
What did we make of the seagulls to become the residents
of wharves and of the saltiness of dry air: welcoming as we bid farewell?
They used to be the proclivity of each river not looking for a constant.
They used to dash in life hoping for a path that saves them from scattering . . .
and because they knew from life only life as it gave
itself, they didn't ask what is after their fates and their graves.
And why should they be concerned with Resurrection?
Why should they care whether Ishmael or Isaac was a ram to the Lord?
This hell is the Hell. They became used to planting their mint in their shirts
and learned to plant lablab ivy around their tents; used
to memorizing the violets in their songs and in the flower pots of their dead . . .
but no harm befell the plants, no harm, when longing embodied the plants.
And they returned before their sunset; to their names
and to the clarity of time in the swallow's travel.

As for places of exile, they are places and times that change their kin
they are the evenings that dangle from windows that look upon no one
they are the arrivals to coasts aboard a ship that has lost its horses
they are the birds that exceed the eulogy of their songs . . . and the land
that belongs to the throne, and abbreviates nature in a body.

But they returned from exile, and if they had left their horses behind
it's because they broke their myths with their hands, to leak out and liberate
themselves and think with their hearts. They returned
from the grand myth to remember their days and their speech.
They returned to the familiar among them as it walks
on the pavement, aimlessly chewing sweet laziness and time,
seeing flowers the way people see them . . . without story
the lemon blossom is born out of the lemon blossom, and in the dark it opens
the windows of ancient houses to the vastness . . . and to the family salaam.

And it seems they have returned.
Because there's enough time for the caravan to return from India's
distant journey. They repaired their carriages and stepped ahead of speech,
and lit up the star of memory in the windows of middle Asia, they returned,
it seems they have returned.
They returned from Syria's north, they returned
from small islands in the generous ocean, returned
from countless conquests and countless captivities, returned
like a minaret to the muezzin's voice at sunset.
The roads didn't mock them as a stranger mocks a stranger.
The river became their obsession, if it stuttered or advanced, receded or flooded.
And a fortune-teller hung the willow banner on what gold flows from the moon.

And they have their story. Adam, their migration's grandfather, cried

in regret, and emigrated to the desert. The prophets were dispersed in every land,
and civilization and palm trees emigrated
but they returned
as caravans

    or vision

       or idea

         or memory
and saw in the old images enough sedition or affliction to describe the end.
Was the desert enough for the Adamic wandering? Adam poured the honey
of the first desire in the uterus, and the apple witnessed. Adam resisted
his death. He lived to worship his high lord, and he worshiped his high lord to live.
Was Cain—the first murderer—aware his brother's sleep was death?
Was he aware Abel hadn't yet learned the names or language?
Was the first woman, the one covered with the berry shirt, a map?
There is no sun under the sun other than the light of these hearts piercing
the shadows. How many epochs have passed to find the answer to the question?
And what is the question if not an answer that has no question?
Those were the questions of sand to sand. A prophecy of what is seen or unseen.
An ignorance claiming prophecy. And the sand is the sand. And the Sufi
sneaks away from a woman to weave the wool
of his darkness with his beard, then ascends as a crystal body and asks:
Does the soul have buttocks and a waist and a shadow?

    In captivity, there is room for the sun of doubt
they are drunkards at the door—their freedom
is what has fallen out of the absolute broken space around their tents:
helmets, tin, blueness, a pitcher of water, weapons,
human remains, a crow, a sand hourglass, and grass covering a massacre.

Can we build our temple on a meter of this earth . . . to worship
the creator of insects, names, enemies, and the secret concealed in a fly?
Can we bring back the past to our present's periphery, to kneel
on our rock to those who have written time in the book without a writing?
Can we sing a song on a heavenly stone to withstand
the myths that we could alter only by interpreting clouds?
Can our aquatic mail reach us on a hoopoe's beak
and bring back our letter from Sheba, to believe in the strange and the legendary?

In wandering there is room for horses to blaze from the slopes to the heights
then drop from the slopes to the bottom; room for horsemen who prod the night
and the night is all night. And death at night is murder.

Anthem! Take all the elements
and take us higher
one era at a time
to see of man's narrative what would bring us back
from absurdity's long journey to the place — our place,
take us higher on the spearheads to overlook the city —
you know the place better
and how strong the things within us are,
and you know the time better . . .

Take me to a stone —
to sit near the distant guitar
take me to a moon —
to know what remains of my wandering
take me to a string —

that pulls the sea to the fugitive land
take me to a journey —
    whose death is small in the artery of oud
take me to a rain —
    on the roof tiles of our lonely house
take me to me so I can belong to my funeral on my festival day
take me to my festival like a martyr in the violet of the martyr . . .
they returned, but I did not . . .
take me there, to there, from the jugular to the jugular.

    They returned to what was in them of homes, and they recovered
the silken foot upon the luminous lakes, recovered
what was lost of their dictionary: the olives of Rome in the imagination of soldiers,
the buried Torah of Canaan under the temple ruins between Jerusalem and Tyre,
the incense road to Quraish blowing from the Syria of roses,
the gazelle of eternity paraded for the Nile's northerly ascension,
paraded for the virility of the savage Tigris that parades Sumer to immortality.
    They were together.
They were warring with one another, conquering and conquered.
They were together.
Marrying and begetting the progeny of antithesis or of madness.
They were together.
Allies against the north, building across hell
the crossing bridge out of hell to the victory of the soul in each of them.
And they recurred in the battle over the mind:
Whoever has no mind in his faith has no soul . . .
Are we able to incarnate creativity from Gilgamesh

who was the dispossessed of immortality herbs,
and from Athena after him? Where are we now!
The Romans must locate my existence
in marble, return to Rome the point of the world, and give
birth to my ancestors out of their superior swords.
But there is that of Athena within us which makes the ancient sea our anthem.
Our anthem is a stone scratching the sun within us,
a stone radiating our mystery. Extreme clarity is a mystery.
How can we realize what we have forgotten?
Christ returned to supper, as we had wished, and Mary returned to him
on her long braids to blanket the Roman theater within us.
Was there enough meaning in the olives . . . to fill Christ's palms
with serenity, his wounds with basil, and pour our souls over him as radiance?

> Anthem, take all the elements
> and take us higher wound by wound.
> Bandage forgetfulness
> and take us as high as you can to the human
> around his first tent
> he shines the dome of the copper horizon
> to see
> what he does not see
> of his heart.
> And take us higher before you descend
> with us to the place,
> you know the place better
> and the time.

And in the passageways they prepared for the siege.

Their camels were thirsty as they milked the mirage

to drink the milk of prophecy from the imagination of the south.

And in every exile, and for their sage plants, there was a citadel with broken gates,

and for every gate a desert completing the narrative

of the long journey from war to war.

And for each boxthorn in the desert there was a Hagar migrating south.

They passed by their chiseled names over the metals and pebbles

but didn't recognize their names . . . victims don't believe their intuition . . .

they didn't recognize their names . . .

names that were erased by sand at times, or covered by the foliage of sunset.

Our history is their history.

And aside from the differences between the birds in the banners,

the nations would have united

the roads of their thoughts. Our beginning is our end . . .

and land

like language

is inherited . . .

and if the two-horned king had one horn,

and if the world were larger, the easterner

would have become easterly in his tablets,

the westerner more estranged.

And if Caesar had been a philosopher

the little earth would have become Caesar's home.

Our history is our history . . .

        and the bedouin may extend his palm tree toward the Atlantic

on the Damascus Road so we can heal from the fatal thirst for a cloud.

Our history is their history.

Their history is our history

      had it not been for the conflict over the timing of Resurrection!

Who united the stubborn land without a sword adorned with valor?

No one ...

Who returned from the journey to the basil of childhood?

No one ...

Who fashioned his narrative far from the rise of its antithesis and heroism?

No one ...

There must be an exile to lay the eggs of memory and abridge eternity

in a moment that encompasses time ...

perhaps all they did was to rewrite their names

and recall, in the silver of olives, the first poet who shrouded their sky:

Aegean Sea! bring us back ... our family dogs have barked

to lead us back to where our wind once blew ... because victory is a death.

And death is a victory in Hercules ... and the martyr's stride is a home.

We are the ones who have come to become victorious ... the oracles cast us

in the north of our estrangement without asking about our wives.

Those who died are dead,

and those who remember their homes kill more of the elderly and the young girls

and toss the city's children from their beds

into the steep valley to return, before time could, from the Troy of the devil;

or did we betray the government of our conscience

for our wives to betray us?

The solid conscience was our crossing bridge,

it was a ship that carried incense to our women, and beautiful perfume to Helen.

And victory, like defeat, is a death, and crime might lead to virtue.

Ancient sea! adorn the murdered with their murderer, and return us
to the barking of our dogs in our first land. But proceed without us
to the adventures of searching for what was lost of our fleet . . . the ancient
fishing boats, and the men who have become coral trees in the depths,
we want to return, from the wars of defending the bed's throne,
to our women's sheets, and to the poplar fabric
that is green in the ashes and in our poets' visions . . .
There must be a land where we can dock our steps and the hazelnut of our houses—
the light, this light, is not enough for us to pluck the berries of our home.

They used to be in dialogue with the waves to mimic those who are coming
back from the battles beneath the arch of triumph. Our exile was not in vain at
all, and we didn't go into exile in vain. Their dead will die without regretting a
thing. And the living can bequeath the calm wind, learn to open the windows, see
what the past makes of their present, and weep slowly and patiently lest the ene-
mies hear the broken ceramics within them. Martyrs, you were right, the road to
the house is more beautiful than the house, despite the flowers' betrayal, but the
windows don't look out on the sky of the heart . . . and exile is exile, here or there.
We did not go into exile in vain at all, and our exile wasn't in vain.

And land
like language
is inherited!

And they didn't resemble the captives, and didn't impersonate the freedom
of martyrs. They weren't rid of the summer of their desolation. Yet they flamed

the faraway mountain with their desolation, then turned absent when they couldn't find roads out of their slopes that dispersed them among the wadis. The first shepherds might reach the echo. They might discover the remnants of their clothes and voices, discover the time of their weapon: their winding flute. From each people they intimated a legend to mimic its heroes, and in each war one of their gallant horsemen died, but the rivers have their directions. And yesterday is no longer a yesterday for them to inhabit a place a little higher than the riverhead . . .

Their guitars are a mare and an Andalus upon my foot
girl of the wind tap us upon needles of pine
and we will love our lives
tap the air with sandalwood
tap us to soften the soul within
and we will leave
the harbor to itself
tap us with the cadence of wine
on the blackness of secret amid
the two whites rid us now of the corals
of your big wadi teach us
the work of joy armed with gypsy blood
tap us with your high heels tap what looks out
of the hearts and the nations
will turn around and notice
the beginning of their wars: a man
searching the prairie for his serenity
resides in a woman.

And on desert and sea waves, they raised an island for their existence.
They returned, and their poet said:
I defend my journey to my destiny as I defend my anthem
among the palm trees and their punctured shadow. Out of my void I will walk
toward being anew, and I will walk away from the bridge—abandon it
to the faraway and to the lemon blossom—the bridge
of the blue that is broken with rain.
So, chanters, cross, if you are able to return
the neighing to the horses, cross.
The horses pant after my heart as it leaps out of my hands toward the dams.
We are who we are, so who will change us? We return and don't return
and march within ourselves,
and when a single morning without death
and a night without dream come,
we will reach the harbor, scorched by the final roses . . .
And it seems they have returned.
The sea descends from their fingers and from the edge of the bed . . .
they used to see their houses behind the clouds
and hear their goats bleat, they used
to palpate the antlers of the gazelles of narrative
and kindle the fire on the hill. They used
to exchange cardamom. Bake the pies of the happy feast.
Do you remember
our estrangement's days over there? They used to dance on the suitcases mocking
the narrative of exile and the countries longing will abandon:
Do you remember the last siege of Carthage?
Do you remember the fall of Tyre

and of the kingdom of the Franks on the Syrian coast, the grand death
in Tigris when ashes flooded the city and the ages?
"Behold, Saladin, we have returned . . ."
so look now for new children.
They used to repeat the story from its end to the age of comedy.
Tragedy might enter comedy one day
and comedy might enter tragedy one day . . .
and in the narcissus of tragedy they mocked
the silver of comedy, and they used to ask and ask:
Of what will we dream when we realize Mary was a woman?
They used to smell the herbs in the walls that commenced their spring
and their wounds, the herbs that brought them back from every exile.
The honeycomb sting resembles a snakebite, and the basil scent
is the coffee of exile . . . a walkway for emotions in their homes . . .
We have arrived!
They clapped for their dogs, for the houses of their return, the grandfathers
of the story, the ancient plows, and the friction of the sea with the onions
that hang on antique weapons. Bygones are bygones.
And the husbands teased the wives of funerals:
We are through with the tears of dancing, lamenting, and weeping,
let's narrate the hearts that gallop with horses to the rising wind of memories,
let's narrate the steadfast Hercules in his final blood and in the mothers' madness,
and let's be him, the Ulysses
of paradox if the sea wished it so, dear women,
let's narrate and narrate, when we narrate, the calling of the Kurd commander
to the hesitant Arab: Give me a sword

and take from me the blessings upon the prophet, his disciples and women,
and keep the alms . . .
    They laughed a lot:
Perhaps prison is prettier than the gardens of exile.
And they saw their windows looking out on their humor
and firing up the roses around the riverbanks.
Bygones are bygones. They will leap unto ladders;
        they will open the safes of memories
            the chests of clothes
                polish the door handles
                    and count their rings;
their fingers had grown bigger with the days and their eye sockets had swelled.
They couldn't find their faces on the rust of mirrors or glass.
That's fine!
The garden will expand when they arrive in a little while before the anthem.
And they will look back:
We are still who we are, who will send us back to the desert?

    We will teach our enemies a lesson in agriculture and in the bursting of wa-
ter from stone . . . we will plant peppers in the soldier's helmet . . . plant wheat on
every slope, wheat is larger than the borders of the reckless empire of any age. We
will follow the habits of our dead and wash off the rust of the years from the silver
of trees . . .

Our country is that it becomes our country
our country is that we become its country

its vegetation, its birds, and its inanimate things
and our country is our birth
our grandfathers
our grandchildren
our livers walking upon intaba or grouse feathers
and our country is that we make a fence of violets for its fire and ashes
it is that it becomes our country
it is that we become its country
a paradise
or an affliction
one and the same—

We will teach our enemies the homing of pigeons, if we can teach them. And we will sleep in the afternoon under the shade of a grapevine trellis, while the cats around us sleep on the drizzle of light. And the horses sleep on their fugitive bending. And the cows sleep and chew grass. Though the rooster is sleepless because of chickens in his life. We will sleep in the afternoon under the shade of a grapevine trellis. We have had enough ... we have tired of the sea air and of the desert—

They used to return
and dream they had arrived
because the sea was descending from their fingers and from the shoulders
of their dead. They used to witness things suddenly:
the sweet basil upon the shrouded hero's final step:
Does he die here with his gun and silk brocade and his final threshold?

Does he die here? Here and now under the noon sun?
It was just now his victory fingers shook
the gate of the old house, and the walls of the island.
Just now he guided the last steps toward the target . . . and concluded the journey
with the return of our dead. Then the sea slept under the windows of small homes.

    O sea! we weren't often wrong . . .
don't give us more than the others . . . we know
the victims within you are countless. And water is a cloud.

    They used to be as they used to be.
They used to return and ask the gloom of destiny: Must there be a hero who dies
to enlarge the vision and add one more star to our banner?
They weren't able to add a rose to the ending,
to change the path of ancient myths:

    the anthem is the anthem:

    there must be a hero who falls on the victory fence

    in the height of anthem.
O hero within us . . . don't rush!
Live one more night for us to reach the end of a life adorned
with incomplete beginning; another night
for us to complete the journey of the bloodied dream,
O crown of our thorns; twilight of the myth that is crowned
with an endless beginning. O hero within us . . . don't rush!
Live another hour
for us to begin the dance of divine victory.
We are not victorious yet, so wait, hero, wait.
Why do you depart

an hour before arrival?
O hero
within us
don't
rush!

     There remains of the exile in them the autumn of confession
there remains in them a street that leads to exile . . .
and rivers that flow without banks
there remains in them a soft narcissus that fears the drought
there remains in them what changes them if they return and do not find:
the same anemones
the same stubborn quince fuzz
the same daisy
the same loquat
the same long ears of wheat
the same elderberry
the same dried garlic braids
the same holm oak
the same alphabet
. . . they were on the verge of descent to the air of their houses . . .
but from which dream should they dream?
With what thing should they enter the garden of doors
while exile remains exile?
     And they used to know the road to its end and to dream.
They came from tomorrow to their present . . . and they used to know
what would happen to the songs in their throats . . . they used to dream

of the carnation of their new exile on the house's fence, they used to know
what would happen to the hawks if they settled in palaces, they used to dream
of the conflict of their narcissus with paradise when paradise becomes their exile,
and they used to know what would happen to the swallow
when spring burns it, they used to dream of the spring
of their obsession, whether it came or not, they used to know
what would happen when the dream arrives from a dream
and knows it was dreaming;

they used to know, and dream, and return, and dream, and know, and return,
and return, and dream, and dream, and return.

THE HOOPOE

We haven't approached the land of our distant star yet. The poem takes us
through the needle's eye to weave, for space, the aba of the new horizon.
We are captives. Even if our wheat leapt off the fence and the swallow burst
out of our broken chains, captives, what we are, what we love and want . . .
But there is a hoopoe within us who dictates his letters to the olive of exile.
Our letters came back to us from our letters, to write anew
what the rain writes of primitive flowers on the stone of distance.
And the journey—the echo travels from and to us. We aren't basil
to return in spring to our little windows. We aren't leaves
for the wind to take us to our coasts. Here or there is a clear line
for wandering. How many years must we raise our dead
as mirrors to the sweet mysterious? How many times
must the wounded carry mountains of salt to find the commandments?
Our letters came back to us from our letters. Here or there is a clear line—
for shadow. How many seas must we cross inside the desert?
How many tablets must we forget?
How many prophets must we kill at noon?
How many nations must we resemble to become—
a tribe? This road, our road, is the reed upon the words that darn the hem
of the aba between our desolation and the earth, and the earth distances itself
to doze off in our saffron sunset. So let's open
like a palm and lift our time to the gods . . .
I am a hoopoe—the guide told the master of things—I search for a lost sky.

We said: What remains of the wilderness is only what the wilderness finds
of us: the remnants of skin over thorn, the warrior's song to home, and the mouth
of space. Our relics are in front of us. And behind us is absurdity's shell . . .
I am a hoopoe—the guide told us—then flew with the rays and the dust.
Then our sages asked about the meaning of story and departure:
Where did we come from when our relics are in front of us,
and the willows behind us? From our names we come
to our names, and we hide forgetfulness from our kids. The stags spring from stags
onto the temples. And the birds lay eggs over the comedy of statues. We didn't ask
why humans weren't born of trees that permit return. The oracles told us
the hearts are weighed on a scale in ancient Egypt. The oracles told us
the obelisk supports the horizon from falling onto the ages. And that we
will repeat our journey there on the outer darkness. And the oracles told us
the kings are our judges, and the witnesses are our foes. And the soul
is guarded by shepherds. Our journey is a bridge between two rivers,
and we weren't born to be erased, though life obliterates . . .
I am a hoopoe—the guide said—I will be guided to the spring if vegetation dries.
We said: We aren't birds. He said: You won't reach Him, all is His,
and all is within Him, He's in everything, search for Him if you want to find Him,
He is within Him. We said: We aren't birds to fly. He said: My wings are my time,
and passion is passion's fire, so burn to cast the place's body off yourselves.
We said: Did you return from Sheba to take us to a new Sheba? Our letters
came back to us from our letters but you didn't return . . . you didn't.
And in Greece you didn't comprehend Aristophanes,
didn't find the city in the city. You didn't
find the house of compassion to wrap us up in the silk of serenity.
You didn't attain the meaning, so the poets' obsession enchanted you: "Fly,

daughters of my feathers, birds of the plains and wadis, fly
swiftly fly toward my wings and toward my voice." There is a yearning
in us to fly in our passions, but humans aren't birds to fly . . .
Hoopoe of words, when you hatch the meaning and the birds
snatch us from language, son of strain, when the butterfly
splits from its elements and feeling resides it, dissolve our clay,
for the light to cleave the image of things. Soar and clarify
the distance between what we were and what will be our final present.
We move away, but end up near our truth and the walls of our estrangement.
Passage is our obsession. We're the duality of earth-sky, sky-earth
and around us are fence and fence. So what's behind the fence?
Adam was taught all the names for the grand secret to bloom,
and the secret is our journey to the secretive. Humans are birds that don't fly . . .
I am a hoopoe—the guide said—and below us is Noah's flood. Babylon.
Petrified remains. The vapor of the nations' call to water.
Skeletons and an end like a beginning to an end.
We said: Soar, for the murderer to forget his victims.
Soar above us. Soar for the creator to forget his creation, his things,
and the names in the myth of creation that we exchange.
—Did you know all this beforehand, hoopoe?
—I knew that a volcano would draw the new image of the universe.
—Yet you, postman of the earth, said nothing. —I tried . . . We know
there are enough ghosts in the hoopoe to make him search in the graveyards
for his beloved . . . he had a mother, and a south that settles on his flight.
He had the myth of speculation that is crowned with water . . . and among his paths
there are a king and a woman . . . and an army guarding the two juvenile bodies

from our dreams. We have enough of the desert
to grant the hoopoe the rein to our mirage and clouds.
We have enough fragility to hand over to him our sleep's sleep.
Take us, hoopoe, our tongues are puzzled, how do we praise
the One who asked for praise when His praise is within Him.
All is within Him for all. We accepted that
we are humans in this desert, and we dissolved into love. Where
is our palm tree so we'll find our hearts in the dates?
And God is more beautiful than the road to God. But those who travel
don't return from a wandering to be lost in another wandering!
They know the road is the arrival at the beginning of the impossible road.
Hoopoe of secrets, struggle, for us to witness our love in the beloved.
It's an eternal journey, this search for the adjective of the One who has no
adjective. His adjectives are free from our description and His traits. Take us high.
What remains of us is our journey to Him. To Him
we plead what we endure in departure . . .
Our blood is His nations' wine over the marble and on the supper table.
Hoopoe, "There is no you but you," so steal us to you if you please, and guide us
one day to the quick earth, before we spin in the bottomless pit, guide us
one day to trees we were secretly born under to hide our shadow,
guide us to childhood. To doves that once faked what they were to disgrace us.
The children grew up but didn't fly like the doves. How we wish. We wish. Perhaps
we'll fly one day . . . humans are birds that don't fly. And the earth
is larger when we're ignorant, smaller when we know our ignorance.
But we're the descendants of this clay, and the devil of fire tries, as we do,
to attain the nearby secrets, to burn us and burn our minds.

Yet the mind is only smoke, let it get lost! The hearts will guide us.

So take us, hoopoe of secrets, to our vanishing through His vanishing.

Take us high then bring us down to bid our mother farewell.

Endlessly waiting for our horses, she wants to die when light breaks, or live

for Nishapur as a widow who adorns our nights.

She "wants only God from God" . . . take us then!

Love is not to attain the beloved, the hoopoe said:

On a flute's echo a lover sent the mare of absence

for his woman and abridged the road and said: I am she. And she

is the "I" unraveling from despair toward hope, to return me to despair.

And my roads to her doors are endless . . . and my "I" flew "so the only I is I . . ."

And the nations' roads to the same old springs are endless!

We said: The canons will become complete

when we get past this archipelago and free the captives from the tablets.

Let the void sit in its arcade so the human in us can complete the migration . . .

Who are these flutes looking for in the forests? We are the strangers.

We are the folk of the abandoned temple, abandoned atop our white horses—

the reed sprouts over us and meteors flash above us, we search for our final station.

There's no earth left where we haven't built an exile for our small tent.

Are we the skin of the earth? Who are the words looking for inside us?

Are these the words that brought us to the court of vision in the underworld?

The words that built the temples to tame its desolate beast with image and psalm?

Our relics are in front of us. And behind us. Here and there. And the oracles

told us: The city worships the ancestors in ancient China. The oracles told us:

The ancestors take their throne to the holy grave—they take

the girls as wives and the war captives as guards. The oracles told us:

Divinity is the twin of man in ancient India. The oracles told us

what the creatures told us: "You are also who He is" . . . although we didn't
raise our fig tree for the comers from the south to hang us on it.
Are we the skin of the earth? We used to bite the rock and open—
a space for the jasmine. We used to seek refuge in God from his guards and wars.
We used to believe what we learned of the words. Poetry used to descend—
from the fruits of our nights, and lead our goats to the pastures on the raisin trail.
The dawn was blue, soft, and moist. And when we dreamt we used to be content
with the borders of our houses: we would see honey on the honeycomb, then
gather it, see the square of a sesame seed complete in our sleep, then sift it, see
what we would see at dawn. Dream was the lover's handkerchief.
But we didn't raise our fig tree for the comers from the south to hang us on it.
I am a hoopoe—the guide replied—then flew . . . and the words flew—
from us. The Flood came before us. We didn't take off the clothes of the earth—
the Flood came before us. We hadn't begun the self wars yet. It came before us.
We hadn't harvested the barley of our yellow fields. It came before us.
We hadn't burnished our stones with a ram's horn, the Flood
came before us. We hadn't despaired of apples. The sad mother would bear
brothers from our flesh, not from the chestnut trunk, nor
from iron. The sad mother would bear brothers to erect the exile
of anthem. The sad mother would bear brothers to dwell
in the palm fronds, if they want, or on the plains of our horses. And she would bear
brothers who anoint Abel king of the throne of dust.
But our journey to forgetfulness has turned long. And the veil ahead of us masks
the veil. Perhaps the mid-road is the road to a road of clouds.
Perhaps we are, hoopoe of secrets, ghosts searching for ruins?
The hoopoe said: Leave your bodies and follow me, leave the earth—the mirage
and follow me. And leave your names. Don't ask me for an answer.

The answer is the road and the only road is to vanish in the fog.
We asked: Are you under the spell of al-Attar?
—He spoke to me then went into the belly of Passion's Wadi.
We asked: Did al-Ma'arri stop by the Wadi of Knowledge?
—His road is the absurd. We asked: And Ibn Sina . . . did he answer
your question and did he see you? —I see through the heart, not through
philosophy. Are you a Sufi then? —I am a hoopoe. I have no want. "I want
not to want" . . . then the hoopoe disappeared into yearning: O love,
you have tormented us. From travel to travel you send us in vain. You have
tormented us and estranged us from our kin, from our water and air. You have
corrupted us. Emptied the hours of sunset from the sunset. Dispossessed us
of our first words. Robbed the peach tree of our days, dispossessed our days. O love,
you have tormented us, and robbed us. Estranged us from all things and veiled
yourself with autumn leaves. You have robbed us, love. Left not a little
thing for us to search for you in it, or to kiss its shadow, so leave
for us an ear of wheat within the soul that loves you more. Don't break the glass
of the universe around our calling. Don't fret. Don't clamor. Be calm
for a while so we can see the elements in you as they lift their total wedding
toward you. Approach us so we can realize for once: Do we deserve
to be the slaves of your hidden shudder? Don't scatter
what remains of our sky's rubble. O love, you have tormented us,
O gift, you have dispersed us to guide our unknown toward rising . . .
this unknown is not ours and the river's mouth is not ours,
and life rises before us like leaves of ancient cypress, to lead
longing toward longing. You have tormented us, love, made us absent
from ourselves, and dispossessed our names . . .
Then, intoxicated, the hoopoe reappeared and said: Fly just to fly.

We said: We're only lovers. We have tired of the whiteness of love, we long
for a mother, a dry land, a parent. Are we who we were and who we'll be?
He said: Unite on every path and vaporize to reach the One
whom the senses cannot reach. Each heart
is a universe of secrets. Fly just to fly. We said: We are only lovers,
we have often died and been elated. We are only lovers. Longing
is exile. Our love is exile. And our wine is exile. And exile
is the history of this heart. We have often said to the scent of the place: Petrify
so we can sleep. We have often told the trees of the place to strip off
the ornament of invasions so we can find the place.
And non-place is the place when its soul becomes remote from its history . . .
Exile is the soul that distances us from our land, toward the beloved.
Exile is the land that distances us from our soul, toward the stranger.
No sword remains that hasn't sheathed itself in our flesh.
And our enemy-brothers saddled the enemy's horses to exit our dreams.
The past is exile: we plucked the plums of our joy off the barren summer.
Thoughts are exile: we watched tomorrow beneath the windows then broke through
our present's walls to reach it, but it became the past in a soldier's ancient shield.
And poetry is exile when we dream then forget where we were when we waken.
Do we deserve a gazelle? Hoopoe of secrets,
take us to our endless tomorrow! Hang our time over the vastness. Take us high.
All of nature is soul, and the earth appears from here
like a breast for the grand shudder, and the horses of wind are our vessel . . .
So birds, O birds, fly just to fly, all of nature is soul. And encircle
your fascination with the yellow hand, your sun, and dissolve. Then turn around
after you've burned, and head toward the land, your land,
to illuminate the tunnel of the solid question about this existence and about

the little wall of time. All of nature is soul, and soul is the body's last dance.

Fly higher than flight . . . higher than your sky . . . just to fly, higher

than the grand love . . . than the sacred . . . than the divine and the sensuous.

Liberate yourself from all the wings of questions about beginning and destiny.

The universe is smaller than a butterfly's wing in the courtyard of the large heart.

In a grain of wheat we met, then parted in bread and in the journey.

Who are we in this anthem that we should roof the desert with this copious rain?

Who are we in this anthem that we should free the living

from the captivity of graves? Fly with your swift wings, birds, on squalls of silk.

You may fly as our elation. The universal echo will call to you: Fly

to attain the flash of vision. But we will descend onto ourselves,

and if we waken, we will return to visit a time that wasn't enough

for our happiness or for the climate of Resurrection.

Who are we in this anthem that we should meet its antithesis as a door to a wall?

And what good is our idea without humans since we are made of fire and light?

I am a hoopoe, the guide replied. And we said: We are a flock of birds, words

are fed up with us and we with them, we're full of thirst, and echo has scattered us.

For how much longer will we fly? The drunkard hoopoe said: Our goal is the vastness.

We said: And what's behind it? He said: Vastness after vastness after vastness.

We said: We're tired. He said: You won't find a pine tree to rest on. What you ask

of descent is in vain, so soar just to soar. We said: How about tomorrow,

we'll fly again tomorrow . . . the earth will still be there, a ripened breast suckled

by the clouds, a gold that scratches the blue shudder around our homes.

The earth has everything—even if we don't know it. We shall return when we return

to see it with our hoopoe's eyes that have possessed our eyes.

Salaam upon the earth, salaam unto it . . .

It has the bed of the universe with cotton sheets made of vision and clouds.

It sleeps on arms of water as owner of its image and ours. And it has
a small moon that combs its shadow like a servant. And the moon passes
among our hearts frightened of exile and of the fate of myth,
then darkness illuminates it like a vigil for the state of the self near the miracles.
Is this what words are born out of, for clay
to become man? Did we know the earth to forget it and forget
the fish of childhood around its navel? Do we see from afar what we don't see
when near? The days were often our fortresses on the string of language.
The rivers were often our flutes though we didn't notice. And the marble
often imprisoned some of our angels but we never knew it. And Egypt and Syria
have often lost their way. There's a land to the land
above which our hoopoe was captive. There's a soul to the land—
the wind scattered it. And Noah didn't leave all the messages for us.
Christ walked to Galilee and the wounds in us clapped. Here, the doves
are the words of our dead. Here, the Babylonian ruins
are a mole in our journey's armpit. Here an apple body swims in the galaxy.
And water is that body's belt as it flows along eternity,
embodied in our eulogies, and then returns to itself
like a mother who covers us with her naked fur of longing, hides what we've done
to the lung and the fire of her rose, hides our journey's war, and what the sword
has done to the map of grass around the shores of the sacred feathers.
Our mother is our mother. The Athenians' mother.
The ancient Persians' mother. Plato's, Zaradasht's, Plotinus's,
Suhrwardi's, and everyone's mother. Each child is a master in his mother.
The beginning and end are hers. As if she is what she desires to be: birth.
And if she desires, she is also the forbidden death.
You fed and nourished us, Mother, to feed our children, so when is the weaning?

O spider of love. Death is a murder. We love you, O how we love you,

grant us mercy. Don't kill us a second time and don't give birth to the serpents

near the Tigris . . . and let us walk on the gazelles of your waist

near your waist, the air is the dwelling place.

Lure us as the mischievous partridge is lured to the nets, and embrace us.

Were you there before our migration?

The passion of wandering changes us into a poem

that has opened its windows so the pigeons can complete the poem

then carry it as a meaning that brings back the sap to the invisible

trees on the banks of our souls . . .

Fly, then, just to fly in the courtyards of this heart, fly.

What good is our idea without the human since we are made of clay and light?

Did you know, hoopoe, what crown was on your head?

The hoopoe replied: My mother's grave. When I fly carrying secrets and news,

my mother is a festival on my head . . .

He's a hoopoe, we said, he's the guide and what's in him is in us, hung by time

like a bell for the wadis. Yet the place becomes narrow in vision and time breaks.

What do you see, hoopoe . . . what do you see in the faraway image of shadow?

—I see the shadow of His image over us, so let's soar to see Him, He is the only He:

"O heart . . . my mother and sister," my wife, pour yourself out to see Him . . .

But after all, our hoopoe, we said, is just a hoopoe . . .

Water has a throne that rises beneath the drought, and the holm oaks rise also.

Water has the color of the field when the zephyr of dawn lifts it on the horses' backs.

Water has the taste of the gift of song lunging from memory's garden.

Water has the scent of the beloved on the marble, increasing our thirst and stupor.

Water has the shape of sunrise brevity when it splits us in two: human and bird.

And our hoopoe has horses of water that rise under his drought as the scepter rises.

And our hoopoe ... has a time he once carried, and he once had a tongue.
And our hoopoe ... has a land he once carried as messages to the distant heavens.
There's no religion the hoopoe hasn't offered to the creatures as a departure to God.
There's no love that hasn't tormented the hoopoe
with breaking through a lover to his other. And the hoopoe is always a traveler.
Who are you in this anthem? I am the guide, he said.
And the hoopoe is always a traveler. Who are you in this anthem?
I am departure, he said. "O heart ... my mother and sister," pour yourself out
so the impossible can see you—and for you to see it,
and take me, both of you, to my final mirror. Our hoopoe said this then flew ...
Are we what we were? There are trees on our ruins and a beautiful moon
in our travel. And we have a life over there in others' lives.
Yet we were coerced into the orphaned Samarkand.
We don't have a king to bring back. The days left
to us what the flute bequeathed of the days ... the nearest of them is farthest.
And we have of rain what the lablab ivy has.
We are now what we were, we have come back
coerced to the myths that didn't expand for our arrival, and we organize
our days around our anthem. And we have temples over there, and here
we have a god whose martyrs praise.
And we have flowers of night musk the day shuts out.
And we have a life in others' lives. We have oil and wheat—
we didn't make our tent out of our willows, we didn't make gods
out of sulfur for the soldiers to come and worship. We found everything
ready: our broken names in the jars
of clay ... our women's tears of old berry stains
on the garments ... our old hunting rifles ... and a previous festival

we can't retrieve. The wasteland is packed with traces of human absence.

And it seems we were here once. It seems

there are enough tools here to pitch a tent above the wind.

And the Flood has no tattoos on the wrinkles of the mountain with green borders.

But there are a thousand nations in us that have passed between song and spear.

We came to learn that we came to return from an absence we don't desire.

And we have a life we haven't yet tried.

And an immortal salt that hasn't immortalized who we are.

And we have steps no one before us has taken . . . so fly,

fly, O birds, in the courtyards of this heart, fly,

and gather around our hoopoe, and fly . . . just . . . to fly!

ELEVEN PLANETS

1992

ELEVEN PLANETS AT THE END

OF THE ANDALUSIAN SCENE

I.

ON THE LAST EVENING ON THIS EARTH

On the last evening on this earth, we sever our days
from our trees, and count the ribs we will carry along
and the ribs we will leave behind, right here . . . on the last evening
we bid nothing farewell, we don't find the time to end who we are . . .
everything remains the same, the place exchanges our dreams
and exchanges its visitors. Suddenly we are incapable of satire
since the place is ready to host the dust . . . here on the last evening
we contemplate mountains surrounding clouds: a conquest and a counterconquest
and an ancient time handing over our door keys to the new time
so enter, you conquerors, our homes and drink our wine
out of our simple muwashah. We are the night when midnight comes, no
horseman carries the dawn from the ways of the final azaan . . .
our tea is hot and green so drink it, our pistachio fresh so eat it,
and our beds are cedar green, so surrender to sleepiness
after this long siege, sleep on our dreams' feathers,
the sheets are ready, the perfume by the door is ready, and the mirrors are many
for you to enter them so we can leave them entire. In a little while
we will search for what was our history around your history in the distant lands
and ask ourselves in the end: Was the Andalus
right here or over there? On earth . . . or in the poem?

HOW DO I WRITE ABOVE THE CLOUDS?

How do I write above the clouds my kin's will? And my kin
leave time behind as they leave their coats in the houses, and my kin
whenever they build a fortress they raze it to erect above it
a tent of longing for the early palm trees. My kin betray my kin
in wars of defending salt. But Granada is gold
and silken words embroidered with almonds, silver tears in
the oud string. Granada is for the great ascension to herself . . .
and she can be however she desires to be: the longing for
anything that has passed or will pass: a swallow's wing scratches
a woman's breast in bed, and she screams: Granada is my body.
A man loses his gazelle in the wilderness and screams: Granada is my country.
And I come from there. So sing for the sparrows to build from my ribs
a stairway to the proximal sky. Sing the gallantry of those ascending to their fate
moon by moon in the lovers' alley. Sing the birds of the garden
stone by stone. How I love you, you, who tore me
string by string on her way to her hot night . . . sing!
There is no morning for coffee's scent after you, sing my departure
from the cooing of pigeons on your knees, and from my soul's nest
in the letters of your easy name, Granada is for song, so sing!

I HAVE BEHIND THE SKY A SKY

I have behind the sky a sky for my return, but I
am still polishing the metal of this place, and living
an hour that foresees the unknown. I know time
will not be my ally twice, and I know I will exit
my banner as a bird that does not alight on trees in the garden.
I will exit all of my skin, and my language.
And some talk about love will descend in
Lorca poems that will live in my bedroom
and see what I have seen of the bedouin moon. I will exit
the almond trees as cotton on the brine of the sea. The stranger passed
carrying seven hundred years of horses. The stranger passed
right here, for the stranger to pass over there. I will soon exit
the wrinkles of my time as a stranger to Syria and the Andalus.
This earth is not my sky, yet this sky is my evening
and the keys are mine, the minarets are mine, the lanterns are mine, and I
am also mine. I am the Adam of two Edens, I lost them twice.
So expel me slowly,
and kill me quickly,
beneath my olive tree,
with Lorca . . .

IV.

AND I AM ONE OF THE KINGS OF THE END

And I am one of the kings of the end . . . I leap off
my horse in the final winter, I am the Arab's last exhalation.
I do not gaze upon the myrtles on the roofs of houses, I do not
look around in case someone here knows me
and knows that I have burnished the marble of speech for my woman
to cross barefoot over the dappled light. I do not look upon the night lest
I see a moon that used to light all of Granada's secrets
one body at a time. I do not look upon the shadow lest I see
someone who carries my name and runs after me saying: Take your name
and give me the silver of white poplars. I do not look around lest
I recall I have passed over this earth, there is no earth
in this earth since time around me broke into shrapnel.
I was not a lover to believe waters are mirrors,
as I once told my old friends, and no love redeems me.
And since I have agreed to the treaty of wandering, there's no present
to help me pass near my yesterday, tomorrow. Castile will raise
her crown over God's minaret. I hear the keys rattle
in our history's golden door, farewell to our history. Or am I the one
to shut the sky's last door? I am the Arab's last exhalation.

V.

ONE DAY, I WILL SIT ON THE SIDEWALK

One day, I will sit on the sidewalk ... the stranger's sidewalk.
I was not a narcissist, still I defend my image
in mirrors. Weren't you, stranger, here one day?
Five hundred years have come and gone, and the rift between us
isn't complete, right here, the letters between us haven't ceased, and the wars
haven't changed my Granada gardens. One day I will pass by her moons
and scratch a lemon with my desire ... Embrace me so I can be reborn
out of sun and river scents on your shoulders, out of two feet
that scratch the evening to shed milk for the poem's night ...
I was not a passerby in the words of singers ... I was the words
of singers, the peace of Athens and Persia, an east embracing a west
in the departure to one essence. Embrace me so I can be reborn
out of Damascene swords hanging in the shops. Nothing is left of me
but my old shield, my gilded saddle. Nothing is left of me
but an Ibn Rushd manuscript, *The Collar of the Dove*, and the translations ...
I used to sit on the sidewalk in the daisy square
and count the pigeons: one, two, thirty ... and count the young girls who
snatch the tree shadows above the marble then leave for me
the leaves of time, yellow. Autumn passed me by and I didn't notice.
All of autumn passed, and our history passed over the sidewalk ...

and I didn't notice!

VI.

TRUTH HAS TWO FACES AND THE SNOW IS BLACK

Truth has two faces and the snow is black over our city.

We are no longer capable of despairing more than we have already,

and the end walks toward the fence confident of its footsteps

on this court that is wet with tears, confident of its footsteps.

Who will lower our flags: we, or they? And who

will dictate to us "the treaty of despair," O king of dying?

Everything has been previously prepared for us, so who will tear our names

from our identities: you, or they? And who will plant in us

the speech of wandering: "We could not undo the siege

so let's hand our paradise keys to the messenger of peace, and be saved . . ."

Truth has two faces, the sacred symbol was a sword for us

and against us, what have you done with our fortress to this day?

You did not fight because you feared martyrdom, but your throne is your coffin

so carry your coffin to keep the throne, O king of waiting.

This departure will leave us like a fistful of dust . . .

Who will bury our days after us: you . . . or they? And who

will raise their banners above our walls: you . . . or

a despairing horseman? Who will hang their bells over our journey:

you . . . or a wretched guard? Everything has been previously prepared for us

so why do you prolong the ending, O king of dying?

VII.

WHO AM I AFTER THE STRANGER'S NIGHT?

Who am I after the stranger's night? I rise from dream
frightened of the vague day over the marble of the house,
and of the sun's darkness in flowers, of my fountain's water,
frightened of the milk on the lips of figs, I am frightened
of my language, of the air combing a willow, frightened
of the clarity of dense time, and of a present no more
a present, frightened of passing by a world that isn't
my world. O despair, be mercy. O death, be
a respite for the stranger who sees the unseen clearer than
a reality no longer real. I will fall from a star
onto a tent on the road . . . to where?
Where is the road to anything? I see the unseen clearer than
a street no longer mine. Who am I after the stranger's night?
I used to walk to the self along with others, and here I am
losing the self and others. My horse on the Atlantic coast disappeared
and my horse on the Mediterranean thrusts the Crusader's spear in me.
Who am I after the stranger's night? I cannot return
to my brothers near the palm tree of my ancient house, and I cannot come down
to the bottom of my pit. O the unseen! There is no heart for love . . . no
heart for love in which I can dwell after the stranger's night . . .

VIII.

WATER, BE A STRING TO MY GUITAR

Water, be a string to my guitar. The new conquerors have arrived
and the old ones have gone. It's difficult to remember my face
in mirrors. Be my memory that I may see what I lost . . .
Who am I after this exodus? I have a rock
that carries my name over hills that overlook what has come
and gone . . . seven hundred years guide my funeral behind the city walls . . .
and in vain time circles to save my past from a moment
that gives birth to the history of exile in me . . . and in others . . .
Water, be a string to my guitar, the new conquerors have arrived
and the old ones have gone south as nations who renovate their days
in the rubble of transformation: I know who I was yesterday, so what
will I become tomorrow under the Atlantic banners of Columbus? Be a string,
water, be a string to my guitar. There is no Egypt in Egypt, no
Fez in Fez, and Syria is distant. And no hawk
in my kin's banner, no river east of the palm trees besieged
by quick Mongol horses. In which Andalus will I end? Right here
or over there? I will know that I perished here and left my best
behind me: my past. Nothing remains for me except my guitar,
O water, be a string to my guitar. The conquerors have gone
and the conquerors have come . . .

IX.

IN EXODUS I LOVE YOU MORE

In exodus I love you more, soon
you will lock up the city. I have no heart in your hands, no
road carries me, and in exodus I love you more.
There's no milk for our balcony's pomegranates after your breasts. The palm trees
are lighter. The weight of the hills is lighter, and the streets are lighter at dusk.
And the earth is lighter as it bids its earth farewell. And the words are lighter,
the stories lighter on the staircase of the night. But my heart is heavy.
Leave it here around your house howling and lamenting the beautiful time,
my heart is my only country, and in exodus I love you more.
I empty the soul of the last words: I love you more.
In departure the butterflies lead our souls, in departure
we recall the shirt button we lost, and forget
the crown of our days, recall the fermented apricot scent, and forget
the horse dance in our wedding nights, in departure
we are the equals of birds, we pity our days, and the little that is enough for us.
Your golden dagger making my murdered heart dance is enough for me.
So kill me, slowly, that I may say: I love you more than what
I said before this exodus. I love you. Nothing hurts me.
Not the air, and not the water . . . There is no basil in your morning, no
iris in your evening that hurts me after this departure . . .

X.

I WANT FROM LOVE ONLY THE BEGINNING

I want from love only the beginning, the pigeons darn
this day's dress over my Granada squares.
There's a lot of wine in the jars for a feast after us.
There are enough windows in the songs for pomegranate blossoms to explode

I leave the Arabian jasmine in the vase, I leave my little heart
in my mother's closet, I leave my dream laughing in water.
I leave the dawn in the honey of figs, I leave my day and my yesterday
in the alleyway to the orange plaza where the pigeons fly

Was I the one who descended to your feet, for speech to rise
as a white moon in your nights' milk . . . Stomp the air
for me to see the street of the flute blue . . . Stomp the evening
for me to see how marble falls ill between me and you

The windows are empty of your shawl's gardens. In a different time
I used to know a lot about you, and pick gardenias
off your ten fingers. In a different time, I had pearls
around your neck, and a name on a ring illuminating darkness

I want from love only the beginning, the pigeons flew
over the sky's last ceiling, the pigeons flew and flew.
A lot of wine will remain, after us, in the jars
and a bit of land is enough for us to meet, and for peace to arrive

THE VIOLINS

The violins cry with gypsies going to the Andalus
The violins cry over Arabs leaving the Andalus

The violins cry over a lost time that doesn't return
The violins cry over a lost country that might return

The violins burn the forests of the faraway darkness
The violins bleed the vastness, and smell the blood in my veins

The violins cry with gypsies going to the Andalus
The violins cry over Arabs leaving the Andalus

The violins are horses on a string of mirage, and on moaning water
The violins are a field of savage lilacs swaying near and far

The violins are a monster that a woman's fingernail tortures
The violins are an army building a cemetery of marble and nahawand

The violins are the chaos of hearts maddened by wind in the dancer's foot
The violins are flocks of birds that flee the lacking banner

The violins are the grievance of wrinkled silk in the lovers' night
The violins are the distant sound of wine over a previous desire

The violins follow me, here and there, to take revenge on me
The violins search for me to kill me, wherever they may find me

The violins cry over Arabs leaving the Andalus
The violins cry with gypsies going to the Andalus

THE "RED INDIAN'S" PENULTIMATE

SPEECH TO THE WHITE MAN

Did I say, The Dead?
There is no Death here,
there is only a change of worlds.

— Duwamish Chief Seattle

1.

Then, we are who we are in the Mississippi. We have what is left to us of yesterday
    But the sky's color has changed, and the sea to the east
has changed, master of white ones! horse master, so what do you want
from those who are going to the trees of the night?
    Our souls are high, our pastures sacred, and the stars
are illuminated speech ... if you stared into them you would read our story entire:
we were born here between water and fire ... and will become reborn
in the clouds at the edge of the lapis coast after Resurrection ... soon.
So do not kill the grass anymore, the grass has a soul in us that defends
the soul in the earth
    Horse master! train your horse to apologize
    to nature's soul for what you have done to our trees:
    Ah! my tree my sister

they have tortured you as they have tortured me

do not ask forgiveness

for the logger of your mother and mine . . .

2.

. . . The white master will not understand the ancient words

here, in spirits emancipated between trees and sky . . .

because Columbus the free has the right to find India in any sea,

and the right to name our ghosts as pepper or Indian,

and he is able to break the compass of the sea then mend it

along with the errors of the northerly wind. But he doesn't believe

humans are equal like air and water outside the map's kingdom!

And that they are born as people are born in Barcelona, though they worship

nature's god in everything . . . and do not worship gold . . .

Columbus the free searches for a language he did not find here,

and for gold in our kind ancestors' skulls, he did

as he pleased with the dead and the living in us. Why then

does he still see this annihilation from his grave to its end?

Nothing remains of us but an ornament of ruin, and light feathers

on the garments of the lakes. You have burst seventy million hearts . . . enough,

enough for you to return from our death as monarch of the new time . . .

isn't it time we met, stranger, as two strangers of one time

and one land, the way strangers meet by a chasm?

We have what is ours . . . and we have what is yours of sky.

You have what is yours . . . and what is ours of air and water.

We have what we have of pebbles ... and you have what you have of iron.
Come, let's split the light in the force of shadow, take what you want
of the night, and leave two stars for us to bury our dead in their orbit,
take what you want of the sea, and leave two waves for us to fish in,
take the gold of the earth and the sun, and leave the land of our names
and go back, stranger, to your kin ... and look for India

3.

... Our names are trees of the deity's speech, and birds that soar higher
than the rifle. Do not sever the trees of the name, you comers
from the sea in war, and do not exhale your horses aflame in the plains,
you have your god and we have ours. You have your faith and we have ours.
So do not bury God in books that promised you a land in our land
as you claim, and do not make your god a chamberlain in the royal court!
Take the roses of our dreams to see what we see of joy!
And sleep in the shadow of our willows to fly like pigeons
as our kind ancestors flew and returned in peace.
You will lack, white ones, the memory of departure from the Mediterranean
you will lack eternity's solitude in a forest that doesn't look upon the chasm
you will lack the wisdom of fractures, the setback of war
you will lack a rock that doesn't obey the rapid flow of time's river
you will lack an hour of meditation in anything that might ripen in you
a necessary sky for the soil, you will lack an hour of hesitation between one path
and another, you will lack Euripides one day, the Canaanite and the Babylonian
poems, and Solomon's songs of Shulamit, and you will lack the lily of longing

you will lack, white ones, a memory that tames the horses of madness
and a heart that scratches the rock to burnish itself on the violins' calling . . .
you will lack the confusion of the gun: if our murder is imperative, then do not
kill the animals that have befriended us, and do not kill our yesterday
you will lack a truce with our ghosts in the barren winter nights
and you will lack a dim sun, a gibbous moon, for the crime to appear
less festive on the movie screen, so take your time
to kill God . . .

4.

. . . We know what this ambiguous rhetoric conceals for us.
A sky descending on our salt pacifies the soul. A willow
walking afoot the wind, a beast founding a kingdom in
the vacuoles of wounded space . . . and a sea salting our wooden doors.
The earth wasn't any heavier before creation, but we knew something
like this existed before time . . . the wind will narrate to us
our beginning and end. Yet today we hemorrhage our present
and bury our days in the ashes of legend. Athena is not ours,
we know your days from the smoke of the place. Athena is not yours,
we know what the master-metal prepared for our sake
and for the sake of gods that did not defend the salt in our bread.
And we know that fact is stronger than truth, that time
has changed when the weapons changed. So who will raise our voices
to a brittle rain in the clouds? Who will wash the light after us
and who will dwell in our temple after us? Who will preserve our rituals

from the metallic roar? "We promise you civilization," the stranger said,
and said: I am the master of time, I have come to inherit your earth,
pass before me, to count you corpse by corpse over the face of the lake.
"I promise you civilization," he said, to revive the gospels, he said, so pass
for God to remain mine alone, dead Indians are better
to the Lord in his heights than living Indians, the Lord is white
and white is this day: you have a world and we have a world . . .
The stranger says strange words, and digs a well in the earth
to bury the sky in it. The stranger says strange words
and hunts our children and the butterflies.
What have you promised our garden, stranger?
Some tin roses prettier than our roses? Do what you please, but do
you know the deer will not chew the grass if our blood touches it?
Do you know the buffalo and the plants are our brothers?
Do not dig the earth any deeper! Do not wound the turtle whose back
the earth, our grandmother the earth, sleeps upon, our trees are her hair,
and our adornment her flower. "There is no death in this earth," do not change
her fragile creation! Do not break the mirrors of her gardens,
or startle her, do not hurt the earth. Our rivers are her waist
and we are her grandchildren, we and you, so do not kill her . . .
We will be gone, in a little while, so take our blood and leave her
as she is,
        as God's most beautiful writing on the water,

                                     leave her for him . . . and for us.
We will hear our ancestors' voices in the wind, and listen
to their pulse in our tree buds. This earth is our grandmother,
all of it is sacred, stone by stone, this land is a hut

for gods that dwell within us, star by star, and illuminate for us
the prayer nights . . . We walked barefoot to touch the soul of pebbles,
and we marched naked for the soul, the soul of the air, to wear us as women
who give back nature's gifts—our history is her history. Time had enough
time for us to be born in her, and return from and to her: we patiently give back
to the earth her souls. And we preserve the memories of our loved ones in jars
of oil and salt, we used to hang their names on the birds of the creeks.
We were the first, there was no ceiling between the sky and the blue of our doors,
there were no horses chewing the grass of our deer in the fields, no strangers
passing through the nights of our wives, so leave a flute behind for the wind to cry
over the wounded people of this place . . . and over you tomorrow,
to cry . . . over you . . . tomorrow!

5.

And as we bid our fires farewell, we don't return the greeting . . .
Don't write the decrees of the new god, the iron god, upon us, and don't ask
the dead for a peace treaty, none of them remain
to promise you peace with the self and others, we had
longevity here, before England's rifles, before French wine
and influenza, we used to live as we should live, companions of the gazelle.
We memorized our oral history, we used to promise you innocence and daisies,
you have your god and we have ours, you have your past and we have ours,
and time is a river, when we stare into the river time wells up within us . . .
Will you not memorize a bit of poetry to halt the slaughter?
Were you not born of women? Did you not suckle as we did

the milk of longing for mothers? Did you not wear wings as we did
to join the swallows? We used to announce spring to you
so don't draw your weapons! We can exchange some gifts and some songs.
My nation was here. My nation died here. Here the chestnut trees
hide my nation's souls. My nation will return as air and light and water,
so take my mother's land by sword, I won't sign my name
to the peace treaty between the murdered and his killer, I won't sign my name
to the purchase of a single hand's breadth of thorn around the cornfields,
I know that I bid the last sun farewell, and that I wrap myself with my name
to fall into the river, I know I will come back to my mother's heart for you
to enter, master of white ones, your age . . . Raise, then, above
my corpse the freedom statutes that do not return the greeting, and chisel
the iron cross on my rocky shadow, I will ascend in a little while the summits
of song, the song of group suicides that parade their history to the far,
and I will release the voices of our birds into them: right here
the strangers conquered salt, the sea merged with clouds, and the strangers
conquered the wheat chaff in us, laid out lines for lightning and electricity,
here the eagle died depressed in suicide, here the strangers conquered
us. And nothing remains for us in the new time.
Here our bodies evaporate, cloud by cloud, into space.
Here our souls glitter, star by star, in the space of song!

6.

A long time will pass for our present to become a past like us.
But first, we will march to our doom, we will defend the trees we wear

and defend the bell of the night, and a moon we desire over our huts.
We will defend the imprudence of our gazelles, the clay of our pots
and our feathers in the wings of the final songs. In a little while
you will erect your world upon our world: from our cemeteries
you will open the road to the satellite moon. This is the age of industry. This
is the age of minerals, and out of coal the champagne of the strong will dawn . . .
There are dead and settlements, dead and bulldozers, dead
and hospitals, dead and radar screens that capture the dead
who die more than once in life, screens that capture the dead
who live after death, and the dead who breed the beast of civilization as death,
and the dead who die to carry the earth after the relics . . .
Where, master of white ones, do you take my people . . . and your people?
To what abyss does this robot loaded with planes and plane carriers
take the earth, to what spacious abyss do you ascend?
You have what you desire: the new Rome, the Sparta of technology
        and the ideology
            of madness,
but as for us, we will escape from an age we haven't yet prepared our anxieties for.
We will move to the land of birds as a flock of previous humans
and look upon our land through its pebbles, through holes in the clouds,
look upon our land through the speech of stars
and through the air of the lakes, through the fragile corn fuzz
and the tomb's flower, through poplar leaves, through everything
that besieges you, white ones, we will look, as dying dead, as dead
who live, dead who return, who disclose the secrets,
so grant the earth respite until it tells the truth, all the truth,
about you
and us . . .

7.

There are dead who sleep in rooms you will build
there are dead who visit their past in places you demolish
there are dead who pass over bridges you will construct
there are dead who illuminate the night of butterflies, dead
who come by dawn to drink their tea with you, as peaceful
as your rifles left them, so leave, you guests of the place,
some vacant seats for your hosts . . . they will read you
the terms of peace . . . with the dead!

A CANAANITE ROCK IN THE DEAD SEA

There is no door the sea opens before me . . .
I said: my poem
is a rock flying to my father as a partridge does. Do you know, Father,
what has happened to me? There is no door the sea shuts against me, no
mirror I can break to scatter the road before me . . . into gravel
or brine . . .
Is there anyone
who would cry over another so I would carry his flute
for him and show what is concealed of my wreckage?
I am a shepherd of salt in the marshes. A bird pecks
my language, and builds his strewn blue nest in my tents . . .
Is there a country
that would ravel from me so I can see it as I want? And so it can see me
by the western coast of my self on eternity's rock?
Father, this is your absence entirely trees
looking upon you from you and from my smoke.
Jericho slept under her ancient palm tree and I found no one
to rock her bed: the caravans have quieted so she can sleep . . .
And I sought a father for my name then a magic wand
split me. Is it my murdered or my vision that rises from my sleep?
And all the prophets are my kin, but the sky is distant
from its land, and I am distant from what I speak . . .
There's no wind here that lifts me higher than the past.

There's no wind that lifts a wave off the salt of this sea, no
banners for the dead to surrender within, and no
voices for the living to trade speeches of peace . . .
And the sea carries my silver shadow at dawn, guides me
to the first words I said to my first woman's breast, then lives dead
in the idolater's dance around his space . . .
and the sea dies alive in the duality of the poem and the sword
between Egypt and Asia and the north . . . so halt your horse,
stranger, beneath our palm tree on the Syrian road!
The strangers will exchange helmets from which basil will sprout,
and the pigeons rising from the houses will spread it to the world.
And the sea died of monotony within bequests that do not die.
And I am I, if you are you over there, I've been a stranger
to the desert palm since the day I was born in this throng.
I am I, there's a war in me and against me . . . so, stranger,
hang your weapon on our palm tree so I may plant my wheat
in Canaan's sacred field . . . Take some wine from my jars,
take a page from my god's scripture . . . and a portion of my food.
Take the gazelle out of our pastoral song's trap, take
a Canaanite woman's prayers on the day of her vineyard's feast, take
our methods of irrigation. Learn from us the lessons of the house. Lay
a baked brick, and erect the pigeon tower above it
to become one of us if you want, a neighbor to our wheat.
And take from us the stars of the alphabet, stranger,
and write with me the messages of heaven
to the nations' fear of nature and of other nations, and leave
Jericho under her palm tree, do not steal my sleep

and my woman's milk, or the sustenance of ants in the marble wound!

Did you come ... then kill ... then inherit

for this sea to gain in salt?

I am I, greener by the year on the holm oak trunk.

This is I, and I am I. And here is my place in my place

and in the past I see you now, as you came, but you don't see me.

And in the past, now, I illuminate for my present

its tomorrow ... then my time moves me away from my place

for a while, and my place moves me away from my time,

and all the prophets are my kin, but the sky is distant

from its land, and I am distant from what I speak. And the sea

descends below the surface of the sea

for my bones to float as trees. My absence is entirely trees.

And my door's shadow a moon. And my mother a Canaanite. And this sea

is a constant bridge for the Resurrection days to pass.

Father, how many times will I die on the bed of a woman of myth

Anat has chosen for me, before a fire rages in the clouds?

How many times will I die in my ancient basins of mint

that your high northerly wind rubs onto letters of doves?

This is my absence, a master reciting his canons

to Lot's descendants and he doesn't see a forgiveness for Sodom besides me.

This is my absence, a master reciting his canons and mocking my vision.

What good is a mirror to a mirror?

I have a face upon you, but you don't

wake from history, you don't wipe the sea mist off yourself.

And the sea, this sea, is smaller than its myth and your hands,

it is crystal's partition, beginning like end ...

There's no meaning here to your absurd entry in a myth
that has abandoned an army to ruins and let a second army narrate
its tale and chisel a mountain for its name. Then a third came
and wrote the story of an adulteress wife, and a fourth
erased the antecedent names. For each army there's a poet
and a historian, and a rababa for the dancers who mock
the beginning and the conclusion . . .
And in vain I seek my absence, simpler than the mules
of prophets passing over the foothills, carrying a heaven for people.
And the sea, this sea, is within the hand's reach. I'll walk upon it
and stamp its silver, grind its salt with my hands. No one
conquers this sea. Khosrau, the Pharaoh, Caesar, Negus,
and the others came to write their names, with my hands, on the tablets
of the sea, so I wrote: This land belongs to my name, this land's name
is what gods share with me on a bench of stone.
I neither went nor came from this gelatinous time
and I am I, even if I broke . . .
I saw my days in front of me golden
on my first trees. I saw my mother's spring, Father, I saw her feather
knitting two birds: one for her shawl, and one for my sister's shawl.
I saw a butterfly that didn't burn in a butterfly for our sake.
I saw for my name a body: I am the male pigeon moaning in the female pigeon.
I saw our house furnished with vegetation, I saw a door for entry
and a door for exit. And I saw a door for entry and for exit . . .
Did Noah pass from one there to another to say
what he said in life: Life has two different doors?
Yet the horse takes me in flight, Father, and takes me

higher, then I fall as a wave that has wounded the valley.

And I am I, even if I broke. I saw my days in front of me,

I saw among my manuscripts a moon that looks upon my darkness.

And I saw an abyss, a war after the war, a tribe whose day

has come and gone, and a tribe that has told the modern Hulagu:

We are yours! But I say: We aren't a slave nation

and I send Ibn Khaldun my admiration.

And I am I, even if I broke on the metal air . . . even if I were handed

over by the new Crusader's war to the god of vengeance.

Or to the Mongol watchman hiding behind an imam's mask.

Or to the women of salt in a myth that has burrowed into my bones . . .

And I am I, if you are my father, yet I've been a stranger

to the desert palm since the day I was born in this throng.

I am I, there is no door the sea opens before me.

I said: My poem

is a rock flying to my father as a partridge does. Do you know, Father,

what has happened to me?

There is no door the sea shuts against me. No mirror I can break

to scatter the road before me . . . into vision . . .

And all the prophets are my kin, but the sky

is distant from its land

and I am distant from what I speak . . .

WE WILL CHOOSE SOPHOCLES

If this autumn is the final autumn, let us apologize
for the ebb and flow of the sea and the memories . . . and for what we have done
to our brothers before the copper age: we wounded many creatures
with weapons made of our brothers' skeletons to extend
their pedigree near the springs. And let us apologize
to the gazelle's kin for what we have done to her near the springs, when
a Tyrian purple thread gushed over the water: we didn't notice it was our blood
historicizing our narrative in the anemones of this beautiful place

And if this autumn is the final autumn, let us unite through clouds
so we can rain for the foliage that hangs over our songs.
Let us rain over the tree trunks of myth . . . and over the mothers who stood
at the beginning of life to retrieve our story from the storytellers
who made the chapters of departure linger.
Were we unable to revise those chapters a little
for the cries of the palm trees to quiet within us?

We were born there on our horses, and we burned with Jericho's ancient sun.
We raised the ceilings of houses for the shadow to wear our bodies. We celebrated
the feast of vineyards and the feast of wheat, and the earth adorned our names
with its lily and its name. And we polished our stones to soften them . . . soften
them in houses brightened by oranges and light, we used to

hang our days in keys of cypress wood. We used to live
gently, living had the taste of small differences among the seasons

And if this autumn is the final autumn, let us move away
from the sky of exile and from others' trees. We grew a little older
and didn't notice the wrinkles in the flute's timbre ... the road lengthened
and we didn't admit we were marching on the path to Caesar. We didn't notice
the poem as it emptied its folk of their sentiments to widen its shores
and pitch our tent where the wars of Athens with Persia,
Iraq with Egypt, tossed us. We love the plow more than
we love the sword, we love the autumn air, we love the rain.
We love nature as it adores the customs of the gods who were born among us
to protect us from the winds of drought and from the horses of an enemy
unknown to us. Yet our doors between Babel and Egypt are open to wars
and open to departure

... And if this autumn is the final autumn, let us abbreviate
our eulogies to ancient urns, where we carved our psalms.
Because others have carved over what we have carved
psalms that haven't been broken yet. The mallow climbs the ancient shields
and its red flowers hide what the sword has done to the name. Our ruins
will turn the shadows green if we are able to reach
our mother at the end of this long tunnel

We have what is ours. Everything is ours: the words of farewell
prepare their ritual ornament for us ... Each word is a woman
by the door guarding the reverberation of echo. Each word is a tree

pounding the lock of vastness with the wind. Each word is a terrace
looking upon dapples of clouds over the empty square
looking upon its shadow over the feathers of cooing . . .

We have what is ours. Everything there is ours . . . our yesterday
prepares our dreams, image by image, refines the manner of our days,
the days of our previous brothers, and of our past enemies,
we are the ones who have burned with the sun of distant lands.
We have come to the first of the earth to follow the previous paths
and possess the previous rose
and utter the previous language.
We will choose Sophocles over Imru' el-Qyss, no matter how the figs
of the shepherds change, or if our previous brothers pray to Caesar
alongside our previous enemies in the banquet of darkness . . .
and no matter how often the narrator's religion changes, there must be a poet
who searches in the crowd for a bird that scratches the face of marble
and opens, above the slopes, the passages of gods who have passed through here
and spread the sky's land over the earth. There must be a memory
so we can forget and forgive, whenever the final peace between us, and between
the wolf and the gazelle, arrives, there must be a memory
so we can choose Sophocles, at the end of the matter, and he would break the cycle.
And there must be a mare over the fields of this neighing . . .

We have in autumn a poem of love . . . a short poem of love.
We revolve with the wind, O love, and fall prisoners near the lake.
We tend to the ailing air, and shake the branches to hear the pulse of air.
We relax the rituals of worship, and leave some gods on either shore

for other nations, then carry the smallest gods and our provisions for the road.
We carry this road ... and walk
and by the springs we study our relics: Have we passed through here?
Are we the owners of this stained glass ... are we who we are?
We will soon know what the sword has done to the name
so leave for us, O love, what is ours ... of the air of the fields

A poem of love is ours in autumn, a short poem of love.
But we could not shorten the life of the road, and our lives
chase us to hurry our steps to the beginning of love. O love, we were
the fox of that fence and the chamomile of these plains. We used to see
what we felt, we cracked our hazelnut on the bell of time, and there was
a solitary road within us to the lunar field, and besides the berries
the night had in it no night, and we had one moon for speech.
We were the storytellers before the invaders reached our tomorrow ...
How we wish we were trees in songs to become a door to a hut, a ceiling
to a house, a table for the supper of lovers, and a seat for noon.
So leave us then for a while, O love, to weave a garb for the beautiful mirage

Our shadow chats with us in the south, and female beasts howl
to a red moon over us. We will touch the bread of the shepherds
and wear the linen of their robes to surprise ourselves ...

                                        those are our days
they pass in front of us in orderly slow steps ...

                                        those are our days
they pass by soldiered vehicles and cast their greeting over the gentle slopes:
Salaam on Canaan's land, land of the gazelle, the purple land

and our days are those . . .

        that unravel thread by thread, and we are the ones
who weave the aba of our days . . . the gods had no role
other than to chat with us, and pour us their wine . . .

            those are our days
they look upon us so we can thirst some more . . . we didn't recognize our wound
in the crowdedness of ancient wounds, but this hemorrhage-place
is called by our names. It isn't our fault we were born here
not our fault . . . that many invaders leapt on us
right here, loved our eulogies to wine, loved our myths
and our olive's silver. It isn't our fault the virgins
of Canaan hung their trousers over stag heads
for wild figs to ripen and for peaches to grow,
not our fault . . . that many narrators came to our alphabet
to describe our land exactly as we did, exactly as we did. Those are our voices
and their voices, they intersect over the hills as an echo to echo.
And the flute mingles with flute, and the wind howls and howls in vain.
As if our songs in autumn are their songs in autumn
as if the land dictates to us what we say . . .
But the barley festival is ours, and Jericho is ours, and we have our habits
in praising our homes and spreading wheat and chrysanthemum

Salaam on Canaan's land,
      land of the gazelle,
          the purple land

RITA'S WINTER

Rita arranges our room's night and says: There isn't much
wine, and these flowers
are larger than my bed
open the window for them to perfume the beautiful night
and place, right here, a moon on the chair, and place
there, on top, the lake around my handkerchief, let the palm trees rise
higher and higher . . .
or have you worn other than me? Has another woman dwelled in you
that you sob each time your branches wrap around my trunk?
Scratch my feet, scratch my blood for us to know what
storms and floods leave behind
of you and me . . .

Rita sleeps in her body's garden
the berries on the fence of her nails light up the salt
in my blood. I love you. Two birds slept under my hands . . .
The noble wheat wave slept on her slow breathing
a red rose slept in the hallway
a night that isn't long slept
and the sea in front of my window slept to Rita's cadence
rising and falling in the rays of her naked chest
so sleep, Rita, in the middle of me and you and don't cover

the deep golden darkness between us
sleep with one hand around echo and the other
scattering the solitude of the forests
sleep between the pistachio shirt and the lemon seat
like a mare upon the banners of her wedding night . . .
The neighing has quieted
the beehives in our blood have died down, but was Rita
here, and were we together?

        Rita will depart in a few hours and leave her shadow
as a white prison cell. Where will we meet?
Her hands asked, but I turned toward the distant.
The sea is behind the door, the desert's behind the sea, kiss me
on my lips—she said. I said: Rita, why should I depart anew
as long as I have grapes and memory, and the seasons still leave me
anxious between gesture and phrase?
—What are you saying?
—Nothing, I mimic a horseman in a song
about the curse of a love besieged by mirrors . . .
—About me?
—And about two dreams on the pillow, they intersect and escape so one
draws out a dagger and another entrusts the commandments to the flute
—I don't get the meaning
—Nor do I, my language is shrapnel
like a woman's absence from meaning, and the horses are in suicide
at the end of the field . . .

Rita sips the morning tea
and peels the first apple with ten irises
and says: Don't read the newspaper now, the drums are the drums
and war isn't my profession. And I am I. Are you you?
I am he, I say
who saw a gazelle throw her glitter upon him
and saw his desires stream after you
and saw the two of us bewildered in unison on the bed
before we became distant like a greeting between strangers on the pier
then departure carried us like a paper in its wind
and threw us at the doorsteps of hotels like letters read in a hurry.
She says: Will you take me with you? I would
become the ring of your barefoot heart
if you take me with you
I would become your garb in a country that birthed you ... to kill you
I would become a coffin of mint that carries your doom
and you would become mine, dead and alive ... ?
O Rita, the guide is lost
and love, like death, is a promise that can't be refused ... and doesn't vanish

Rita prepares the morning for me
like two partridges that have gathered around her high heels:
Good morning, Rita
like blue clouds for the jasmine under her armpits
Good morning, Rita
like fruit for the light of dawn: O Rita, good morning, Rita
bring me back to my body for the pine

needles to quiet briefly in the blood I abandoned after you. Whenever
I embrace the ivory tower two doves flee my hands . . .
She said: I will return when the days and the dreams change. But Rita . . . this
winter is long, and we are who we are, so don't say what I tell myself: I am she
who saw me hanging on the fence, brought me down, bandaged
and washed me with her tears, and spread her lily over me
until I passed among her brothers' swords and her mother's curse. I am she
so are you you?

      Rita gets up
from my knees, visits her beauty, and binds her hair with a silver
butterfly. The horsetail dallies with the freckles that are scattered
like the drizzle of a dark light over the feminine marble. Rita returns
the shirt button to the vinegary shirt . . . and says: Are you mine?
I am yours, I say, if you leave the door open to my past, mine
is a past I see born out of your absence
out of the squeaking time in this door's key, mine
is a past I now see sitting near us like a table
and the soap lather is mine
      the salted honey
        the dew
          and the ginger
Rita says: And yours are the stags, if you want, the stags and the plains
and yours are the songs, if you want, the songs and the astonishment
I was born to love you
a mare who makes a forest dance, and carves your unknown in corals
I was born a woman to her man, take me and I will pour you in the glass

of my final wine, and cure myself of you, in you, so come and bring your heart
I was born to love you
I left my mother in the ancient psalms cursing your people and the world
I found the city guards feeding your love to the fire
and I was born to love you

Rita cracks the walnut of my days, and the fields expand
and this small earth becomes mine, like a room on the ground floor
in a building on a street on a mountain
that overlooks the sea air. I have a moon of wine, and I have a burnished stone.
A share in the scene of the waves that travel in clouds is mine. A share
in the scripture of creation is mine. A share in Job's book, and in
the harvest fest. A share in what I owned, and in my mother's bread.
A share in the lily of the valley in the poems of ancient lovers
and a share in the wisdom of love: the murdered adores his murderer's face . . .
— O Rita, if only you would cross the river?
— And where is the river?
— In you and me there is one river
and I flow as blood and memory
but the guards left no door through which I can enter
so I leaned on the horizon
and looked below
    above
        around
            yet couldn't see
a horizon, I found only my gaze in the light
bouncing back to me. I said: Come back, and I might

see someone looking for a horizon a prophet renovates
with a message of two small sounds: I and you
are a little joy in a narrow bed . . . a small joy
they haven't killed yet, O Rita . . . Rita, this winter
is heavy and cold

Rita sings alone
to the mail of her distant northerly estrangement: I left my mother alone
near the lake, alone, crying over my distant childhood
where each evening she sleeps on the little braid of mine that she has kept.
But, Mother, I broke my childhood and came out a woman nourishing her breast
with the lover's mouth . . .
Rita circles around Rita alone and says:
There is no land for two bodies in one, no exile for exile
in these small rooms, and exit is entry:
We sing between two chasms in vain . . . we should depart and clarify the path
yet I can't and you can't . . . she used to say and not say
while calming the mares in her blood: Is it from a faraway land
that the swallows come, O stranger and lover, to your lonely garden?
Take me to a faraway land
take me to the faraway land, Rita sobbed, this winter
is long . . .
And she broke the ceramic of the day against the iron windowpane
placed her handgun on the poem's draft
threw her stockings on the chair, and the cooing broke . . .
then she went barefoot to the unknown, and departure reached me

A HORSE FOR THE STRANGER

(FOR AN IRAQI POET)

I prepare, to elegize you, twenty years of love. You were alone
over there furnishing an exile for the lady of zizyphus, and a house
for our lord in the heights of speech. Speak so we can ascend higher
and higher . . . on the ladder of the well, my friend, where are you?
Step forward, and I will carry speech for you . . . and elegize you

. . . If it were a bridge we would have crossed it. But it is home and the chasm.
And to the Babylonian moon on the night trees a kingdom no longer
ours, since the Tatars went back on our horses. And the new Tatars
drag our names behind them through mountain limbs, they forget us
and forget the palm trees and the two rivers in us: they forget the Iraq in us

Didn't you tell me on the way to the wind: Soon
we will load our history with meaning, the war will be extinguished soon,
and soon we will rebuild Sumer in the songs
and open the theater doors for people and birds of every sort?
And we will return to where the wind brought us from . . .

. . . There is no room left in the land for the poem, my friend
but is there room left, in the poem, for the land after Iraq?
Rome besieges the rain of our world, and drubs its moons

like copper for jazz. Rome brings time back to the cave. Rome
lunges at the earth, so open another exile for your exile . . .

We have rooms in August's garden, here in the lands that love
dogs more than they love your people and the name of the south. We have
the remnants of women who were expelled from daisies. We have friends
in the kind gypsies. We have the steps to the Tavern. Rimbaud is ours. And we
have the pavement of chestnut. We have the technology to kill Iraq!

The wind of your dead blows southerly. You ask me: Will I see you?
I say: You will see me murdered on the five o'clock evening news
so what good is my freedom, O statues of Rodin? Don't ask, and don't
hang my memory on the palm dates like a bell. We have lost
our exiles since it blew southerly, the wind of your dead . . .

. . . There must be a horse for the stranger to follow Caesar or
to return from the sting of the flute. There must be a horse for the stranger,
or were we unable to see a single moon that doesn't lead
to some woman? Were we unable
to distinguish between sight and vision, my friend?

We have what is upon us of bees and words. We were created to write
about the threats of women, Caesar, and the land when it becomes
a language,
and about Gilgamesh's impossible secret, in order to escape our age.
We went to our yesterday's golden wind, marched to the life span of our wisdom,
and the songs of longing were Iraqi. Iraq is the palm trees and the two rivers . . .

I have a moon in Rasafah. I have fish in the Tigris and the Euphrates.
I have a reader in the south. I have the stone of the sun in Nineveh.
I have the Nairuz in a Kurdish woman's braids in the north of grief.
And I have a rose in the gardens of Babel. I have a poet in Bowaib.
And I have my corpse beneath the sun of Iraq

My dagger is on my image, and my image is on my dagger. And whenever
we're far from the river, my friend, the Mongolian passes between us
as if poems were the clouds of myth. East is not east
and west is not west. Our brothers united in Cain's instinct. So don't
reproach your brother, the violet is the grave's headstone . . .

. . . A grave to Paris, London, Rome, New York, Moscow, and a grave
to Baghdad. Was it her right to believe in her anticipated past?
And a grave to the road's Ithaca and the difficult goal, a grave to Jaffa . . .
A grave to Homer and al-Buhturi, and a grave is poetry, a grave
of wind . . . O stone of the soul, our silence!

We believe, to fulfill the wandering, that autumn has changed within us.
Yes, we are the leaves of this pine, we are the fatigue
as it eased outside our bodies like dew . . . poured out
white seagulls that look for the poets of apprehension within us
and for the Arab's last tears . . . a desert, a desert

. . . There isn't a single bird left in our voice for departure
to Samarkand or to another, because time has broken and language has broken.
And this air we have carried one day on our shoulders

like grapes from Mosul looks upon us like a cross.
So who will carry the poem's burden for us now?

And no voice ascends, no voice descends, soon
we will empty our last utterance into the eulogy of place, and soon
we will gaze into our tomorrow, behind us, in the silk of ancient speech.
And we will watch our dreams searching for us in the hallways
and for the eagle of our black banners . . .

A desert for sound, a desert for silence, a desert for the eternal absurdity
and for the tablets of scriptures, for schoolbooks, for prophets, scientists
and for Shakespeare a desert, for those searching for God in the human.
Here the last Arab writes: I am the Arab who never was
I am the Arab who never was

Say now that you were wrong, or don't say.
The dead will not hear your apology, and will not read
their murderers' magazines to see what they see, and will not return
to the eternal Basra to know what you made
of your mother, when you noticed the blue of the sea . . .

. . . Say we didn't travel to return . . . or don't say.
Because the final say was told to your mother, in your name:
Do you have what proves that you are my only mother?
And if these days are inevitable, let them be the graveyard
they are, and not a transfigured Sodom

The dead will not forgive those who stood, like us, perplexed
at the edge of the well asking: Was Joseph the Sumerian our brother, our
beautiful brother, to snatch the planets of this beautiful evening from him?
And if his murder is inevitable, let Caesar be
the sun over murdered Iraq!

I will become born of you and you of me. I will slowly remove
the fingers of my dead from you, their shirt buttons, and birth certificates,
and you will remove from me the letters your dead sent to Jerusalem.
We will wipe our eyeglasses clean of the blood, my friend, and return
to reading Kafka and open two windows on shadow street . . .

. . . My exterior is in my interior. Do not believe in the winter smoke too much.
April will come out of our sleep soon. My exterior is my interior.
Disregard the statues . . . An Iraqi girl will embroider her dress
with the first almond blossom, then write your initials
above her name on the tip of the arrow . . .
                                        in the rise of Iraq

MURAL

2000

This is your name
a woman said
and disappeared in the spiraling corridor

I could see the sky over there within my grasp.
A dove's white wing carried me toward
another childhood. I wasn't dreaming
that I was dreaming. Everything was realistic. I knew
I was tossing myself to the side
before I flew. I would become what I want
in the final orbit. Everything was white:
the sea hanging above the roof of a white
cloud was nothingness in the white
sky of the absolute. I was
and I wasn't. I was alone in the corners of this
eternal whiteness. I came before my time and not
one angel appeared to ask me:
"What did you do, there, in life?"
And I didn't hear the chants of the virtuous
or the sinners' moans, I was alone in whiteness,
alone . . .

Nothing hurts me at Resurrection's door.
Not time or emotion. I don't feel

the lightness of things or the heaviness
of obsession. I found no one to ask:
Where is my "where" now? Where is the city
of the dead, and where am I? There is no void
in non-place, in non-time,
or in non-being

It's as if I had died before now . . .
I know this vision and know that I
am heading to an unknown. Maybe
I'm still alive in some place, where
I still know what I want . . .

One day I will become what I want

One day I will become an idea. No sword will carry it
to the wasteland and no book . . .
like a rain on a mountain that has cracked
from a single sprout
so neither force
nor fugitive justice can win

One day I will become what I want

One day I will become a bird and unsheathe my existence
out of my void. When the two wings burn
I'll near the truth and reincarnate

from ash. I am the dialogue of dreamers. I turned
away from my body and my self to complete
my first journey toward meaning, but meaning
burned me and disappeared. I am absence.
The heavenly and the expelled

One day I will become what I want

One day I will become a poet,
water will be my vision's subject, and my language
a metaphor for metaphor. I'd neither say nor point
to a place. Place is my sin and pretext.
I come from there. My here leaps
from my steps to my imagination . . .
I am who I was and who I will be,
the endless vast space makes me
and destroys me

One day I will become what I want

One day I will become a vineyard,
so let summer press me from now,
let those passing by the sugary chandeliers
of the place drink my wine.
I am the message and the messenger.
The mail and the tiny address

One day I will become what I want

This is your name
a nurse said
and disappeared in her corridor's whiteness:
This is your name, remember it well!
And don't disagree with it over a letter
or concern yourself with tribal banners,
be a friend to your horizontal name,
try it out on the dead and the living, teach it
accurate pronunciation in the company of strangers,
and write it on one of the cave's rocks
and say: My name, you will grow when I grow,
you will carry me when I carry you,
a stranger is another stranger's brother.
We will seize the feminine with a vowel promised to the flutes.
My name, where are we now?
Answer me. What is now, what is tomorrow?
What is time or place,
the old or the new?

One day we will become what we want

The journey did not begin, nor the road end.
The sages have not attained their estrangement
just as the strangers have not attained their wisdom.
And of flowers we only know the anemones.

So let's go to the highest mural:
My poem's land is green, high,
the speech of God at dawn,
and I am the distant,
the far

In each wind a woman toys with her poet:
Take the direction you gave me,
the one that broke,
and bring back my femininity:
nothing remains for me outside pondering
the lake's wrinkles. Take my tomorrow from me
and bring back my yesterday then leave us alone.
Nothing, after you, will depart
or return

And the poet says: Take my poem if you want,
there's nothing in it for me besides you,
take your "I." I will complete exile
with the messages your hands have left for the doves.
Which one of us is "I" that I may become its other?
A star will fall between speech and writing,
and memory will spread its thoughts: we were born
in the age of the sword and the mizmar
between figs and cactus. Death was slower then.
Clearer. The truce of pedestrians by the river's end.
But now, the electronic button works unaided. No

killer listens to the killed, and no martyr
recites his will

Which wind brought you, woman?
Say your wound's name and I'll know the roads
on which we'll get lost twice.
Every pulse in you aches in me and returns me
to a mythic time. My blood hurts me.
Salt hurts me, and my jugular vein . . .

In the fractured urn the women of the Syrian coast
wailed from the distance
and burned with the August sun. I saw them
on the road to the springs before my birth. I heard
the water in the ceramic jars cry over them:
Go back to the cloud and mirth will return

Echo said:
Only the past of the powerful returns
on the obelisks of vastness . . . (their relics are golden,
golden). While the letters the weak write to tomorrow
return and ask: Give us the bread of sustenance, give us
a stronger present. We are not immortal (we have only
impersonation and incarnation)

Echo said:
I am tired of my intractable hope. I am tired

of the ruse of aesthetic: What after
Babylon? Whenever the road is clearer
and the unknown reveals
an ultimate goal, prose disseminates in prayer
and anthem breaks

Green, my poem's land is green and high . . .
It looks out on me from the flatland of my abyss:
You're strange in your meaning. It's enough
that you be there, alone, to become a tribe . . .
I sang to weigh the spilled vastness
in the ache of a dove
and not to explain what God says to man.
I am not a prophet to claim a revelation
and declare my abyss an ascent

I am the stranger, with all of what I was given
of my language. If I submit my emotion to the *Dhād*,
my emotion submits me to the *Ya'*.
And the words, when far, have a land that neighbors
a higher planet. And the words, when near,
have an exile. The book is not enough for me to say:
I found myself as present as a filled absence.
Whenever I searched for myself I found
the others. Whenever I searched for the others I found
only my stranger self in them,
so am I the one, the multitude?

I am the stranger. Tired from the Milky Way
to the beloved. Tired from my adjectives.
Form has become narrow. Speech wide. I overflow
my vocabulary's need, I look
at myself in mirrors: Am I he?
Do I perform my role well in the final act?
Did I read this script before the show
or was it imposed on me? Am I he
who performs the role, or did the victim change
his affidavit to live the postmodern moment,
since the author strayed from the script
and the actors and spectators have gone?

I sat behind the door watching:
Am I he?
This is my language. And this voice is the prick
in my blood but the author is another . . .
I am not from me, if I come and don't arrive.
I am not from me, if I say and don't speak.
I am the one to whom the mysterious letters say:
Write, and you'll be.
Read, and you'll find.
And if you want to speak then act, and unite
your opposites in meaning . . .
your translucent interior is the poem

There are sailors around me but no port.
Dust has emptied me of gesture and phrase.
I found no time to know where I should settle
my brief moment between two points. I haven't
yet asked my question about the blurred simile
between two doors: entry or exit . . .
And I found no death to snipe at life,
no voice that shouts: Fast time!
you snatched me from what
the mysterious letters of the alphabet say to me:
The realistic is the certain imaginary

Time that has not waited . . .
has not waited for anyone who was late for his birth,
let the past be new, it's your only memory
among us, when we were your friends
and not your vessels' victims. Leave the past
as it is, not leading or led

I saw what the dead remember and forget.
They don't grow older, they don't tell the time
by their wristwatches. They don't feel
our death or their life, and nothing
of what I was or will be. All pronouns
dissolve. He is in "I" and in "you."
Not part and not whole. No living
tells the dead: become me

. . . and all the elements and emotions dissolve. I don't
see my body over there, I don't feel
the ardor of death or my first life.
As if I am not of me. Who am I? Am I
the missing or the newborn?

Time is zero. I didn't think of birth
when death flew me to nebulae,
where I was neither alive nor dead,
where there's no being or void

My nurse would say: You are much better today!
Then she'd inject me with sedatives: Be calm
and worthy of what you're about
to dream . . .

I saw my French doctor
open my cell
and beat me with a stick,
with the help of two policemen from the suburbs

I saw my father coming back
from Hajj, unconscious,
with heatstroke from Hejaz,
saying to a file of angels around him:
Extinguish me . . .

I saw Moroccan youth
playing soccer
and stoning me: Go back with your phrase
and leave our mother here for us,
dear Father, you have lost your way to the grave

I saw René Char
sitting with Heidegger
two meters from me,
they were drinking wine
not looking for poetry . . .
the conversation was a beam of light
and a passing tomorrow was waiting

I saw my three friends weeping
while weaving
with gold threads
a coffin for me

I saw al-Ma'arri kick his critics out
of his poem: I am not blind
to see what you see,
vision is a light that leads
to void . . . or madness

I saw a country embrace me
with morning hands: Be

worthy of the scent of bread. Be
fit for summer flowers,
your mother's brick oven
is still blazing, her greeting
is still warm like the loaf she bakes . . .

Green, my poem's land is green. One river is enough for me to whisper to the but-
terfly: O sister. One river is enough to seduce the ancient myths to remain on the
wings of an eagle. An eagle that changes banners and distant peaks, where armies
have founded the kingdoms of forgetfulness for me. There is no nation smaller
than its poem. But weapons widen the word for the dead and the living in it, and
the letters brighten the sword that hangs in dawn's belt, and the song either dimin-
ishes or expands the desert

There isn't enough life to pull my end toward my beginning. The shepherds took
my story and infiltrated the grass that grows over the beauty of ruins. They over-
came forgetfulness with trumpets and radiant rhymed prose, then bequeathed me
the hoarseness of memory on farewell's stone and didn't return . . .

Our days are pastoral, pastoral, between city and tribe. I did not find a private night
for your howdah that is laureled with mirage. Yet you said to me:

> What need do I have for my name without you? Call to me. I created
> you when you named me, and you killed me when you owned the
> name . . . how did you kill me while I am the stranger of all this night?
> Bring me inside the forest of your desire, embrace me, press me, and

spill this pure processional honey over the honeycomb. Scatter me
with what your hands own of the wind then gather me. Because the
night surrenders its soul to you, stranger, and each star that sees
me knows my family will kill me with the water of lapis lazuli. So —
as I shatter my urn with my hands — bring me in, and I would have
my happy present . . .

. . . or did you say something to me that would change my path?
— No. My life was outside me. I am one who talks to himself:
My last mu'allaqah fell off my palm trees.
I am the traveler within me, besieged
by dualities, but life
is worthy of its mystery
and of the house sparrow . . .
I wasn't born to know that I would die, I was born to love
the content of God's shadow.
Beauty takes me to the beautiful,
and I love your love as it is, liberated
from itself and its adjectives.
I am my alternate . . .

I am one who talks to himself:
from the smallest things the largest things are born,
and cadence doesn't come from the words
but from the aloneness of two bodies
in a long night . . .

I am one who talks to himself
and tames the memory . . . are you me?
And our third flutters between us:
"Don't the two of you forget me, you hear?" Death!
take us, but in our style: we might learn illumination . . .
There is no moon or sun upon me,
I left my shadow stuck in a boxthorn's twigs
before the place became lighter in me
and my fugitive soul took me in flight

I am one who talks to himself:
Woman, what did yearning do to us?
The wind polishes us and carries us like the scent of autumn.
You have grown older on my cane,
you can now get on "the Damascus road"
confident of your vision . . . A guardian angel
and two doves flutter over the remainder of our lives,
and the earth is a festival . . .

The earth is the festival of losers (and we belong to them). We come from the
traces of the epic anthem of the place, and our tents in the wind are an elderly fal-
con's feather. We were kind here, austere without Christ's instructions. We were
stronger than the herbs only at the end of summer:

> You are my truth, and I am your question.
> We inherited only our names.
> You are my garden, and I am your shadows
> at the crossroads of the epic anthem . . .

We didn't participate in the chores of goddesses who used to begin their song with magic and deceit. They used to carry the place on the stag's horns from the time of place to another time . . . we would have been ordinary had our sky's stars been a little higher than the stones of our wells, had the prophets been less insistent, and the soldiers not heard our eulogies . . .

Green, my poem's land is green,
the lyricists carry it from one time to another faithful to its fertility.
And of it, I have
the narcissus contemplating the water of its image.
And of it, I have
the clarity of shadows in synonyms, and the precision of meaning.
And the similarity in the speech of prophets on the surface of night.
And of it, I have the donkey of wisdom forgotten on top of the hill
mocking the poem's reality and myth . . .
And I have the congestion of symbol with its opposites:
embodiment doesn't bring it back from memory
and abstraction doesn't raise it to the grand illumination.
And I have the other "I"
writing its diaries in the notebooks of lyricists:
"If this dream is not enough
then I have a heroic wakeful night at the gates of exile . . ."
And of it, I have echo as it scrapes the sea salt
of my language off the walls
when I'm betrayed by an archenemy of a heart . . .

Higher than the marshes in Aghwar was my wisdom
when I told the devil: No. Don't test me. Don't place me

in the dualities and leave me
as I am, at ease with the Old Testament's narrative,
ascending toward heaven: There is my kingdom. So take
History, son of my father, take it . . . and make
of instinct what you will

And I have serenity. A small grain of wheat
is enough (for me and my enemy brother).
My hour hasn't arrived yet. Nor has
harvest. I must shadow absence
and believe my heart first, follow it
to Cana in Galilee. My hour hasn't arrived yet.
Perhaps there's something in me that banishes me, perhaps
I am other than me. The fig orchards haven't ripened
around the girls' dresses. The phoenix
feather hasn't yet birthed me. There's no one there
waiting for me. I came before, I came
after, but found no one who believes what I see.
I am the one who saw. I am
the distant and the far

Self, who are you? On the road
we are two, and in Resurrection one.
Take me to the light of vanishing to see
what becomes of me in my other image.
Who will I be after you? Is my body
ahead of you or behind you? Who am I?

Form me as I formed you, paint me
with almond oil, crown me with cedar.
Carry me from the wadi to a white
eternity. Teach me life in your style, test me
as an atom in the upper world.
Help me with the boredom of immortality,
and be merciful
when you wound me, when from my arteries
the roses bloom . . .

Our hour hasn't arrived. There are no messengers
measuring time with the last fistful of grass:
whether time has turned around.
And no angels are visiting the place, for the poets
to leave their past on the beautiful dusk
and open their tomorrow with their hands.
So sing, my favorite goddess, Anat, sing again
my first poem about creation . . .
The narrators might find the willow's birth
certificate under an autumn stone. The herders might find
the well in the depths of song. And life might come suddenly,
to those disinclined to meaning, from the wing of a butterfly
caught in a rhyme, so sing, my noble goddess. Say:
I am the prey and the arrow,
I am the words, the one who commemorates,
I am the muezzin and the martyr . . .

I didn't bid the ruins farewell. I was
what I was only once. I was only once:
enough for me to know how time breaks
like a bedouin's tent in the northerly wind.
And how place is cleaved and wears the past,
the scattering of the abandoned
temple. What's around me
resembles me a lot but I resemble nothing
here. As if the earth is too narrow
for ailing lyricists, the devil's grandchildren
who are helpless mad: whenever they see
a beautiful dream they coach the parrot some love
poems before the borders open

And I want to live . . .
I have work to do aboard the ship. Not
to rescue a bird from our hunger or from
seasickness, but to watch the flood
from up close . . . Then what? What
do the survivors do with the ancient earth?
Do they repeat the story? What's the beginning
or the end? No dead
ever came back to tell us the truth . . .

Death! wait for me outside the earth,
in your country, until I finish
some passing talk with what remains of my life

near your tent. Wait for me until I finish
reading Tarafah. The existentialists
tempt me to exhaust every moment
with freedom, justice, and the wine of the gods . . .

Death! wait for me, until I finish
the funeral arrangements in this fragile spring,
when I was born, when I would prevent the sermonizers
from repeating what they said about the sad country
and the resistance of olives and figs in the face
of time and its army. I will tell them: Pour me
in the *Nūn*, where my soul gulps
Surat al-Rahman in the Quran. And walk
silently with me in my forefathers' footsteps,
and on the flute's stride in my eternity.
Don't place violets on my grave: violets are
for the depressed, to remind the dead of love's
premature death. Place seven green ears
of wheat on the coffin instead, and some
anemones, if either can be found. Otherwise, leave the roses
of the church to the church and the weddings.
Death, wait, until I pack my suitcase:
my toothbrush, my soap,
my electric razor, cologne, and clothes.
Is the climate temperate there?
Do conditions change in the eternal whiteness
or do they remain the same in autumn

as in winter? Is one book enough
to entertain me in timelessness, or will I need
a library? And what's the spoken language there:
colloquial for all, or classical Arabic?

. . . Death, wait, wait
until I recover my mind's clarity in spring,
and my health, so you'll be a noble hunter
who doesn't hunt the doe near the water spring. Let the relation
between us be friendly and open: you have of my life
what's yours when I fill it up . . .
and of you I have contemplating the stars and the planets:
no one's ever completely died. Those are souls
that change their residence and form.
Death, my shadow that leads me,
the third of two, the color
of hesitation in emerald and chrysolite,
peacock blood, sniper of the wolf's
heart, imagination's illness—have a seat
on the chair and set your hunting tools
aside under my window. Hang your heavy keys
on the house door and don't stare
at my arteries to detect the final
weakness. You are stronger than
the medical establishment. Stronger than
the respiratory system and powerful honey,
and you don't need my disease to kill me.

Rise above insects. Be yourself,
transparent, a clear mail to the unknown.
Be, like love, a storm on trees, and don't
sit on doorsteps like a beggar or a tax
collector. Don't be a traffic policeman in the streets. Be strong,
with radiant steel, and take off your fox's mask. Be
knightly, beautiful, with thorough blows. And say
what you want. Say: "From meaning to meaning I come.
Life is a flow I intensify and define
with my sultanate and scale" . . .

Death, wait, have a seat.
Have a glass of wine and don't
negotiate with me. The likes of you don't negotiate
with anyone, and the likes of me don't object
to the servant of the unknown. Take a rest . . . perhaps
the star wars have tired you today? Who am I
in their midst that you visit me? Do you have time to test
my poem? No. This is not your concern.
You are responsible for the clay
in the human, not for what he says or does.
Death, all the arts have defeated you, all of them,
all the songs in Mesopotamia have defeated you,
the Egyptians' obelisk, the Pharaohs' tombs,
the carvings on temple rock, all have defeated you,
and immortality has escaped your traps . . .
So do with us, and with yourself, what you will

And I want to live, I want to live . . .
I have work to do in the geography of the volcano.
From Lot's days to Hiroshima
the wasteland has been the same. As if I live here
forever with a lust for what I don't know.
Maybe "now" is farther than I think. Maybe
yesterday's closer. And tomorrow is past.
But I pull "now" by the hand so History
(not the circular time) can pass near me
like the chaos of mountain goats. Will I
survive the speed of electronic time tomorrow,
or will I survive the slowness of my caravan
across the desert? I have work to do for my end,
as if I would not be alive tomorrow. And I have work to do
for an eternally present day. That's why I listen, patiently,
to the sound of ants in my heart:
Aid me against my skin. I listen to the imprisoned
stone's scream: Free my body. I see
in the violin the migration of longing from a land
of dust to a heavenly land. I arrest in the feminine hand
my domestic eternity: I was created,
I loved, got bored, then I wakened
in grass over my grave that tells of me
from time to time. What good is the handsome
spring if it doesn't serenade the dead and complete
life's joy and the lush of forgetfulness after?
This is a method in solving the riddle of poetry,

my sentimental poetry at least, and sleep
is but our method of speech.

Death, have a seat and enmesh yourself
with the crystal of my days, as if you were one
of my constant friends, exiled among
exiled creatures . . . Yet you are the only exile. Don't live
your life. Your life is only my death. You neither
live nor die, and you snatch the children
from the thirst of milk to milk. Though you were
never a child whose bed the swallows rocked,
and no cherubs ever dallied with you, not even
the horns of a distracted stag. But all this happened
to us, we, the guests of the butterfly.
You are the only exile, poor you! No woman
embraces you between her breasts, or shares with you
a longing that abbreviates the night with lewd utterance
as a synonym of the earth's mingling
with heaven within us. And you bore no child
to entreat you and say: Father,
I love you. You are the only exile, O king
of kings, your scepter has no eulogies. No
eagles on your horse. No pearls stud your crown.
You are naked of the banners
and the holy trumpet.
How do you walk like this without guards or a singing choir,
like a coward thief, while you are who you are,

the aggrandized, custodian of the dead, powerful
commander of the obdurate Assyrian army?
So do with us, and with yourself, what you will

And I want, I want to live and forget you . . .
forget our long relationship
so I can read the letters
the distant heavens inscribe. Whenever
I prepared myself for your coming,
you grew more distant. Whenever I said: Go away!
I want to complete the cycle of two bodies in one
that overflows itself, you appeared in the midst of me
and mocked me: "Don't forget our appointment . . ."
—And when is it?
—At the height of forgetfulness, when you believe in life
and piously worship the wood of temples and the drawings
in the cave, when man says: "My relics are who I am
and I am my self's son . . ." so where shall we meet?
—Would you permit me to choose a café by the sea gate?
—No . . . no, son of Adam, son of sin, don't come
near God's borders, you were not born to ask, but to act . . .
—Death, be a kind friend. Be an intellectual meaning: I may realize
the essence of your concealed wisdom. You might have been hasty
in teaching Abel archery. You might have hesitated
before schooling Job in prolonged patience. And you might
have saddled a horse for me to kill me on it. As if my language,
when I remember forgetfulness, can rescue

my present. As if I were forever present. Forever
a bird. As if my language, since I've known you,
has become addicted to its fragility on your white vehicles,
higher than the clouds of sleep,
when feeling is liberated from the burden
of all the elements. Because you and I on God's road
are two Sufis who are governed by vision
but don't see.

Death, go home alone, safe and sound,
I am free here in no here and no there. Go back
alone to your exile. Go back to your hunting tools
and wait for me by the sea gate. Prepare
some red wine for me, to celebrate my return
to the diseased clinic of the earth. Don't be vulgar
with a crude heart! I won't come to mock you, or walk
on the lake's water in the soul's north. But I, now
that you have tempted me, have neglected the poem's end:
I did not parade my mother to my father
on my horse. I left the door open
for the Andalus of lyricists, and chose to stand
on the almond and pomegranate fence, shaking
the spiderwebs off my grandfather's aba
while a foreign army was marching
the same old roads, measuring time
with the same old war machine . . .

Death, is this History:
your brother or your enemy climbing
between two chasms? A dove might build its nest
and lay its eggs in metal helmets. And the woodworm might
grow on the wheels of a shattered vessel.
What does History, brother or enemy, do
with nature, when the earth weds the heaven
and the holy rain is shed?

Wait for me, Death, by the sea
gate in the romantics' café. Your arrows
have missed once, yet I returned only to store my interior
in my exterior. And to spread the wheat that has filled my soul
over the thrush that has alit on my hand and shoulder.
I bid farewell to the land that absorbs me like salt then scatters me
like grass for the horse and gazelle. Wait
while I finish my brief visit to time and place,
and don't believe me if I return or not.
And to life, I say: Thank you!
I was neither dead nor alive,
and you, Death, were alone and lonely . . .

My nurse says: You used to hallucinate
often and scream: Heart,
O heart, take me
to the bathroom . . .

What good is the soul if my body
is ill and unable to perform
its primary function?
Heart, O heart, trace my steps back to me,
I want to walk to the bathroom
on my own.
I forgot my arms, legs, knees,
and the apple of gravity.
I forgot my heart's function
and Eve's garden at the beginning of eternity.
I forgot my little organ's function,
forgot how to breathe with my lungs.
I forgot speech,
I fear for my language:
Leave everything as it is, heart,
and bring life back to my language . . .

My nurse says: You used to hallucinate
often and scream at me:
I don't want to return to anyone,
I don't want to return to any country
after this long absence . . .
I want only to return
to my language in the distances of cooing

My nurse says:
You would hallucinate for a long while and ask me:

Is death what you are doing to me now
or is it the death of language?

Green, my poem's land is green and high ...
Patiently, I write it down, patiently, to the meter
of seagulls in the book of water. I write it
and bequeath it to those who ask: To whom do we sing
when saltiness spreads in dew? ... Green, I write it to the scattering
of wheat ears in the book of the field. A pale fullness
in it and in me has bent it into a bow. And whenever
I befriended a grain spike
or became its brother, I learned from vanishing, and in spite
of it, how to survive: "I am the grain
of wheat that has died to become green again.
And in my death there is a kind of life ..."

And I seem to be and not be.
No one died over there on my behalf.
What, then, do the dead memorize of words
other than those of gratitude: "God is merciful to us" ...
And I entertain myself with remembering what I forgot
of eloquence: "I did not bear a boy to bear his father's death" ...
I preferred the free marriage between words ...
the feminine will find the suitable masculine
in poetry's leaning toward prose ...
then my organs and limbs will grow on a sycamore,
my heart will pour its earthly water

in one of the planets . . . Who am I after I die?
Who am I before I die? Some marginal specter
replied: "Osiris was
like you and me, and Mary's son was
like you and me. Still, at the right moment, the wound
hurts the ill void, and lifts up the temporary
death like an idea . . ."
What is the source of the poetic, the sentimental?
Is it the heart's intelligence or the instinct of sensing
the unknown? Or is it a red rose
in the desert? The personal is not personal.
The universal not universal . . .

And I seem to be and not be . . .
Whenever I listen to the heart I become filled
with what the unknown says, and the trees
lift me high. From dream to dream
I fly without a final goal.
For thousands of romantic years I used to be born
in a darkness of white linen,
I couldn't tell exactly who I was
from my dream. I am my dream.

And I seem to be and not be . . .
my language bid its pastoral tone farewell
only during the migration to the north. Our dogs
were calm. Our goats were veiled with fog

on the hills. And a stray arrow split the face
of certainty. I tired of what my language
on the backs of horses says or doesn't say
about the days of Imru' el-Qyss,
who was scattered between Caesar and rhyme . . .

Whenever I turn my face toward my gods,
over there, in the purple lands, a moon
Anat encircles, illuminates me. Anat
is the lady of metonymy in story. She didn't cry for anyone,
she cried for her beauty:
      Is all this wondrous magic mine alone?
      Is there no poet who shares with me
      my bed's vacant glory
      or picks from my feminine fence
      what overflows of my roses?
      Is there no poet who seduces
      the night's milk in my breasts?
      I am the first
      and the other,
      my limit has exceeded my boundaries.
      And after me the gazelles run in the words,
      there is no one before or after me . . .

I will dream . . . not to mend the vehicles of the wind
or a malfunction in the soul.
The myth has already taken its place—the ruse

in the context of the realistic. And neither can the poem
alter a past that passes or doesn't pass,
nor can it halt the earthquake.
But I will dream.
Perhaps some country is wide enough for me just as I am:
one of the people of this sea
who has ceased asking the difficult question: "Who am I
right here? Am I my mother's son?"
Doubts don't fence me in, and shepherds and kings
don't besiege me, and my present, like my tomorrow, is with me.
My small notebook is with me: whenever a bird rubs wings
with a cloud, I write it down: dream has released
my wings. I too fly. Every living thing
flies. And I am me,
nothing else

And I am one of the people of these plains . . .
in the barley festival I visit my beautiful ruins,
a tattoo in identity
the wind neither kills nor immortalizes . . .
And in the feast of vineyards I gulp
a glass of wine from street vendors . . . my soul
is light, and my body is heavy with memory and place.
In spring, I become a fleeting thought for a tourist woman
who writes on a postcard: "To the left
of the abandoned theater there's a lily and a mysterious
person. To the right, a modern city"

I am me, nothing else . . .
I am not one of Rome's followers, not a sentry
on the roads of salt. But I pay a percentage
of my bread's salt, coerced, and say to History:
Decorate your trucks with slaves and meek kings, and pass . . . no one
says no anymore

I am me, nothing else.
One of this night's people. I dream
of ascending higher with my horse
to follow the water spring behind the hill:
     Persist, my horse, we no longer differ in the wind . . .
     you're my youth and I'm your imagination. Straighten
     like an *Aleph*, and stomp the lightning. Scratch the pans of echo
     with desire's hoof. Rise, renew yourself, and stiffen
     like an abandoned banner in the alphabet.
     We no longer differ in the wind, straighten up
     like an *Aleph*, fret and don't fall off the final slope.
     You're my pretext, and I'm your metaphor
     away from riders who are tamed like destinies.
     Dash and dig my time in my place, horse. The place
     is the road, and there is no road beside you,
     and the wind is your shoe. Illuminate
     the stars in the mirage. Illuminate the clouds in absence,
     and be my brother and my lightning's guide.
     Don't die before me, horse, or after me, or with me
     on the final slope. And look inside the ambulances,
     stare at the dead . . . I might still be living

I will dream . . . not to mend any outer meaning,
but to renovate my abandoned interior from the trace
of emotional drought. I have memorized all of my heart,
like the back of my hand: it's no longer meddlesome
and spoiled. One aspirin suffices to soften
and tranquilize it. As if it were my stranger neighbor.
I am not subject to its whim and women. The heart
rusts like iron and doesn't moan, yearn for, or become
mad over the first tender licentious rain,
it doesn't ring from drought like August grass.
As if my heart were austere, or extraneous
to me like the "like" in a simile.
When the heart's water dries up, the aesthetic
is more abstract, and emotions wrap themselves
in coats, virginity, and talent

And whenever I turned my face toward the first
songs I saw the trace of sand grouse
on the words. I wasn't a happy child to say:
Yesterday is always prettier.
But memory has two light hands that kindle
the land with fever. Memory has the scent
of a crying night flower that wakens in an exile's blood
his need for a chant: "Be my sorrow's
ascension and I will find my time" . . . I need only
a seagull's flutter to follow the ancient ships.
How much time has passed since

we've discovered the twins: time
and natural death, the synonyms for life?
Yet we still live as if death aims at us
and misses us, and we who can remember
are able to liberate ourselves and follow
Gilgamesh's green footsteps
from one epoch to another

All creation is dust, in vain . . .
and absence breaks me like a small water urn.
Enkidu slept but didn't wake. My wings slept
wrapped in a fistful of his clay feathers. My gods
are the inanimate wind in imagination's land. My right arm
is a wooden stick. And the heart is abandoned
like a dried well where beastly echo
widens: Enkidu, my imagination is no longer
enough to finish my journey. I must have force
for my dream to be real. Give me my weapons
and I will polish them with the salt of tears. Bring the tears,
Enkidu, for the dead among us to cry
over the living. What am I? Who is the one sleeping now,
Enkidu? I or you? My gods
are like gripping the wind. So rise within me with all
your human recklessness, and dream of a small
equality between the gods of heaven and us. We are
the ones who build the beautiful earth between
the Tigris and Euphrates, and we memorize the names. How

did you become bored with me, my friend, and let me down?
What good is our wisdom without youth . . . what good is it?
At the entrance of the labyrinth you let me down, my friend,
and killed me, and it has become my duty to see
our destinies. Alone I carry life
on my shoulder like a raging bull. Alone,
with wandering steps, I search
for my eternity. I must solve this riddle, Enkidu, I will
carry for your life what I can, as much
as my strength and resolve will allow. Otherwise,
who am I alone? All creation is dust, in vain
around me. Yet I will prop up your naked shadow
on the palm trees. Where is your shadow?
Where is it after your trunks have been broken?

     The height
     of man
     is an abyss . . .

I was unjust to you when I resisted the beast in you
with a woman who offered you her milk . . . you drank
and were merry, you surrendered to the good omen. Enkidu,
be kind to me and come back from where you died, we might
find the answer . . . for who am I alone?
One's life is incomplete, and I lack
the question, so who will I ask about crossing
the river? Get up, brother of salt,

and carry me. Do you know you're asleep
when you're sleeping? Get up, enough sleep!
Move before the sages accumulate like foxes
around me and say: "Everything is vain, win
your life for what it is, a brief impregnated
moment whose fluid drips
grass blood. Live for your day not
for your dream. Everything will vanish. Beware
of tomorrow and live life now in a woman
who loves you. Live for your body
not for your fantasy, and wait
for a boy who will carry your soul for you.
Because immortality is reproduction in being.
And everything is vain or vanishing
or vanishing and vain"

Who am I?
The Song of Songs
or the university's wisdom?
Both of us are me . . .
and I am a poet
and a king
and a sage on the well's edge,
no cloud in my hand,
no eleven planets
on my temple,
my body is fed up with me,

my eternity is fed up with me,
and my tomorrow
is sitting on my chair
like a crown of dust

Vanity, vanity of vanities . . . everything
on the face of the earth is a vanishing

The winds are northerly
and the winds are southerly,
the sun rises from itself
and sets in itself,
nothing's new,
and time
was yesterday,
in vain, in vain.
The temples are high,
the wheat is spiking high,
and the sky, when it's low, rains,
and the lands, when they rise, are desolate,
and everything that exceeds its limit
becomes its own opposite one day.
And life on earth is a shadow
we don't see . . .

Vanity, vanity of vanities . . . everything
on the face of the earth is a vanishing

1,400 vehicles
and 12,000 horses
bear my gilded name
from one epoch to another . . .
I lived as no other poet has lived,
a king and a sage . . .
I have aged, and I am bored with glory,
there's nothing I lack.
Is this then why
the more I know
the more my burden amasses?
What is Jerusalem and what's the throne?
Nothing remains as it is: there is
a time for birth,
a time for death,
a time for silence,
a time for speech,
a time for war,
a time for peace,
a time for time,
and nothing stays as it is . . .
the sea will drink each river,
and the sea is not full,
nothing stays as it is,
each living creature moves toward death,
and death is not full,
nothing remains except my gilded name after me:

"Solomon was" ...
What will the dead do with their names?
Does gold illuminate
my vast darkness?
Would the Song of Songs
or the university
illuminate my vast darkness?

Vanity, vanity of vanities ... everything
on the face of the earth is a vanishing ...

And as Christ walked on the lake,
I walked in my vision. But I came down
from the cross because I have a fear of heights and don't
promise Resurrection. I only changed
my cadence to hear my heart clearly.
The epicists have falcons, and I have
The Collar of the Dove, an abandoned star on the roof,
and a winding street that leads to Akko's port,
no more and no less.
I want to cast the morning greeting
to myself where I left myself a happy boy
(I wasn't a lucky boy, but distance,
like two skilled ironsmiths,
can forge a moon out of petty iron).
—Do you know me?
I asked the shadow near the wall,

then a girl wearing fire noticed and asked:
Are you talking to me?
I said: I am talking to my twin ghost.
She mumbled: Another Majnoon Laila
is checking in on his ruins. Then she left for her shop
at the end of the old market . . .
We were right here. Two palm trees were carrying
letters of some poets to the sea . . .
We didn't age that much, my "I" and me. The maritime
scene, and the wall that defends our defeat,
and the scent of musk, all say: We're still here,
even if time separates from place.
And maybe we were never apart . . .
— So do you know me?
But the boy I lost cried:
We never parted, though we never met . . .
And he shut two sea waves within his arms
and soared high . . . So I asked:
Which one of us is the immigrant?

Then I met the prison warden by the western coast:
I asked: Are you the son of my first warden?
— Yes.
Where's your father?
— He died a few years ago. He became
depressed from the boredom of his watch
then bequeathed me his profession and task, and admonished

me to guard the city from your song ...
I said: How long have you been watching me
and imprisoning yourself in me?
—Since you wrote your early songs.
I said: You weren't even born then.
—I have a time and an eternity,
and I want to live to America's cadence
and on Jerusalem's wall. .
I said: Be who you are. But I have gone.
The one you see now isn't me, I am my ghost.
—Enough. Aren't you echo's
stony name, you neither went nor came,
and you're still
within this yellow prison cell
so leave me alone.
I said: Am I still here? Am I free or imprisoned,
unawares? And is the sea behind this wall mine?
—You're a prisoner, a prisoner
of yourself and your longing. And the one you see now
is not me. I too am my ghost.
So I said to myself: I am alive, then.
If two ghosts meet in the desert,
do they share the sand
or compete over the monopoly of night?

Akko's port clock was the only thing working.
No one cared about the time of night. The fishermen

were casting their nets for seafood, and braiding
the waves. And the lovers were at the clubs.
And the dreamers were petting the sleeping larks
and dreaming . . .
I said: If I die, I'll pay attention . . .
I have enough past
but I lack tomorrow . . .
I will walk on the old road over
my steps, on the sea air, without a woman
watching me from her balcony, without a memory
except for what's useful for the long journey.
There was always enough tomorrow
in the days. I was younger than
my butterflies and her two dimples:

> Girl, take sleepiness from me and hide me
> in the narrative and the sentimental evening /
> hide me beneath one of the two palm trees /
> teach me poetry / I might learn
> wandering in Homer's ways / I might
> add the description of Akko to the story /
> the oldest beautiful city /
> the loveliest old city / a stone box
> where the dead and the living move
> in its clay as if in a captive beehive /
> laborers who strike against flowers and ask
> the sea about the emergency exit
> when the siege tightens / teach me poetry /

a woman might need some song
for her faraway / and she might say:
Take me to you, even if against my will,
and place my sleep in your hands /
and they'd go to echo in an embrace /
As if I have wed a fugitive doe
to a gazelle / as if I have opened the church
doors to the doves / teach me
poetry / A woman who wove the wool
shirt and waited at the door
deserves some talk about vastness / about
disappointment, and says: The warrior
did not come back, or won't, and you
are not the one I waited for . . . /

And as Christ walked on the lake,
I walked in my vision. But I came down
from the cross because I have a fear of heights and don't
promise Resurrection. I only changed
my cadence to hear my heart clearly . . .

The epicists have falcons, and I have
The Collar of the Dove, an abandoned star on the roof,
and a winding street that leads to the port . . .
And this sea is mine,
this humid air is mine,
this sidewalk and my steps

on it, my semen . . . mine.

And the old bus station. And mine

is my ghost and his companion. And the copper pot,

the Throne verse, and the key are mine.

And the door, the guards, the bells are mine. Mine

is the horseshoe that flew

over the walls . . . and what was mine

is mine. And the piece of paper that was torn

out of the Gospel is mine. The salt of tears

on the house walls, mine . . . and my name,

even if I mispronounce it

with five horizontal letters, is mine:

Meem / the infatuated, the orphaned, the finale of what has passed.

Hā / the garden and the beloved, two puzzles and two laments.

Meem / the adventurer, the readied and ready for his death,

the one promised exile, and desire's ill patient.

Wāw / farewell, the middle rose, loyal to birth wherever possible,

and the pledge of parents.

Dal / the guide, the road, the tear of a meadow that has perished, and a house

sparrow that spoils me and bleeds me . . .

this name belongs to me and my friends

wherever they are . . .

and my temporary body, absent or present, is mine:

two meters of this dirt will suffice . . .

175 centimeters are mine . . .

and the rest belongs to flowers with chaotic colors

that drink me slowly, and what was mine

is mine: my yesterday. And what will be mine:
my distant tomorrow, and the return of the fugitive soul
as if nothing had happened,
as if nothing were
a scratch wound on the arm of the frivolous present . . .
and History mocks its victims
and its heroes . . .
it glances at them then passes . . .
and this sea is mine,
this humid air is mine,
and my name,
even if I misspell it on the coffin,
is mine.
But I,
now that I have become filled
with all the reasons of departure,
I am not mine
I am not mine
I am not mine . . .

EXILE

2005

I. TUESDAY AND THE WEATHER IS CLEAR

Tuesday, clear weather, I walk on a side road
covered by a ceiling of chestnut trees, I walk lightly
as if I have evaporated from my body, as if I have
a meeting with one of the poems. Distracted,
I look at my watch and flip through the pages
of faraway clouds in which the sky inscribes
higher notions. I turn matters of my heart over
to walnut trees: vacancies, without electricity,
like a small hut on a seashore. Faster, slower, faster
I walk. I stare at the billboards on either side
but don't memorize the words. I hum
a slow melody as the unemployed do:
    "The river runs like a colt to his fate / the sea, and the birds
      snatch seeds from the shoulder of the river."
I obsess and whisper to myself: Live
your tomorrow now. No matter how long you live you won't
reach tomorrow . . . tomorrow has no land . . . and dream
slowly . . . no matter how often you dream you'll realize
the butterfly didn't burn to illuminate you.

Light-footed I walk and look around me
hoping to see a simile between the adjectives of my self
and the willows of this space. But I discern
nothing that points to me.

If the canary doesn't sing
to you, my friend . . . know that
you are the warden of your prison,
if the canary doesn't sing to you.

There is no land as narrow as a pot for roses
like your land . . . and no land as wide
as a book like your land . . . and your vision
is your exile in a world where shadow
has no identity or gravity.

You walk as if you were another.

If I could speak to anyone
on the road I would say: My privacy is what
doesn't lead to me, and it isn't a dream
of death. If I could speak to a woman
on the road I would say: My privacy doesn't
draw attention: some calcified arteries
in the feet, that's all, so walk
gently with me as a cloud walks:
"Neither linger . . . nor hurry . . ."

If I could speak to the ghost of death
behind the dahlia fence, I would say: We were born
together as twins, my brother, my murderer,
my road engineer on this earth . . . this earth
is my mother and yours, so drop your weapon.

And if I could speak to love, after lunch,
I would say: We were the panting of two hands
over the lint of words, when we were young,
we were the fainting of words on two knees.
And you were with few features, many

movements, and clearer: your face an angel's
face waking from sleep, your body
ram-strong like a fever. And you used to be called
what you were, "Love," and we
would swoon with night.

I walk lightly and grow older by ten minutes,
by twenty, sixty, I walk and life diminishes
in me gently as a slight cough does.
I think: What if I lingered, what
if I stopped? Would I stop time?
Would I bewilder death? I mock the notion
and ask myself: Where do you walk to
composed like an ostrich? I walk
as if life is about to amend its shortcomings.
And I don't look behind, for I can't return
to anything, and I can't masquerade as another.

If I could speak to the Lord I would say:
God! Why have you forsaken me?
I am only your shadow's shadow on earth,

how could you let me fall into the trap of questions:
why the mosquito, O God?

I walk without a rendezvous, vacant
of my tomorrow's promises. I remember that I forgot,
and I forget as I remember:

I forget a raven on an olive branch
and remember an oil stain on my pants.

I forget the gazelle's call to his mate
and remember the ant line on the sand.

I forget my longing for a star that has fallen from my hand
and remember the fur of a fox.

I forget the ancient road to our house
and remember a passion like mandarin.

I forget the things I've said
and remember what I haven't said yet.

I forget my grandfather's stories and a sword on a wall
and remember my fear of sleep.

I forget a young woman's grape-filled lips
and remember the scent of lettuce on fingers.

I forget the houses that inscribed my narrative
and remember my identity card number.

I forget grand events and a destructive shake of earth
and remember my father's tobacco in the closet.

I forget the roads of departure to a deficient void
and remember the light of planets in the bedouin atlas.

I forget the whizzing of bullets in a village that is now deserted
and remember the cricket sound in the shrub.

I forget as I remember, or I remember that I forgot.

But I remember today,
Tuesday
and the weather is clear.

And I walk on a street that doesn't lead
to a goal. Maybe my steps would guide me
to an empty bench in the garden, or
to an idea about the loss of truth between the aesthetic
and the real. I sit alone as if I had a meeting with one
of imagination's women. I imagine that I waited for long,
got bored with waiting, then exploded when she arrived:
Why were you late?! She lies and says:
It was too crowded on the bridge, settle down . . .

So I settle down as she fondles my hair, and I feel
the garden is our room and the shadows our curtains:

> If the canary doesn't sing
> to you, my friend . . . know that
> you have overslept
> if the canary doesn't sing to you.

What are you saying? she asks.
I say: The canary didn't sing to me, but do you
recall who I am, stranger? Do I resemble the ancient
pastoral poet whom the stars crowned as king of the night . . .
the one who renounced his throne when the stars
sent him as a shepherd for clouds?

She says: If today resembles yesterday,
you seem to be you . . .

> There, on the opposite wooden bench,
> waiting crumbles a young woman
> who cries
> and drinks a glass of juice . . .
> She brightens the crystal of my small heart
> and carries for me the emotions of this day.

I ask her: How did you get here?
She says: By chance. I was walking

on a street that doesn't lead to a goal.
I say: I walk as if I have a rendezvous . . .
maybe my steps would guide me to an empty bench
in the garden, or to an idea about the loss of truth
between the imaginary and the real.
She asks: So you, too, recall who I am, stranger?
Do I resemble yesterday's woman, that young one
with a braid and short songs about our love
after a good long sleep?

I say: You seem to be you . . .

    Over there a boy enters
    through the garden gate
    carrying twenty-five irises
    to the woman who has waited for him.
    He carries, instead of me, the youth of this day:
    This heart, my heart, is small
    and the love, my love, is large.
    It travels in the wind, descends,
    loosens a pomegranate then falls
    in the wandering of two almond
    eyes, then ascends in the dawn
    of two dimples and forgets
    the way back to house and name.
    This heart, my heart, is small
    and the love is large . . .

Was he the one I was
or was I the one I wasn't?

She asks: Why do the clouds scratch the treetops?
I say: For one leg to cling to another beneath the drizzle.

—Why does a frightened cat stare at me?
—For you to put an end to the storm.

—Why does the stranger long for his yesterday?
—For poetry to depend on itself.

—Why does the sky become ashen at twilight?
—Because you didn't water the flowers in the pot.

—Why do you exaggerate your satire?
—For song to eat a bit of bread every now and then.

—Why do we love then walk on empty roads?
—To conquer the plentitude of death with less death and escape the abyss.

—Why did I dream I saw a sparrow in my hand?
—Because you're in need of someone.

—Why do you remind me of a tomorrow I do not see you in?
—You're one of eternity's features.

—You will walk alone to the tunnel of night when I'm gone.

—I will walk alone to the tunnel of night when you're gone.

. . . and I walk,

heavy as if I have an appointment with one of the defeats.

I walk, and a poet in me readies himself for his eternal rest

in a London night: My friend on the road to Syria,

we haven't reached Syria yet, don't hurry, don't make the jasmine

a bereaved mother, or test me with an elegy:

how do I lift the poem's burden off you and me?

The poem of those who don't love describing fog

is his poem.

The coat of the clouds over the church

is his coat.

The secret of two hearts seeking Barada

is his secret.

The palm tree of the Sumerian woman, mother of song,

is his tree.

And the keys of Córdoba in the south of fog

are his keys.

He doesn't append his name to his poems,

the little girl knows him

if she feels the pinpricks

and the salt in her blood.

He, like me, is haunted by his heart,

and I, like him, don't append my will to my name.
And the wind knows my folks' new address
on the slopes of an abyss
in the south of the distant . . .

Farewell, my friend, farewell, and bid Syria salaam.
I am no longer young to carry myself
upon the words, no longer young
to finish this poem . . .

And at night I walk with the *Dhād*, my private language, I walk
with the night in the *Dhād*, an old man urging
an aging horse to fly to the Eiffel Tower: O my language,
help me to adapt and embrace the universe. Inside me
there's a balcony no one passes under for a greeting.
And outside me a world that doesn't return the greeting.
My language, will I become what you'll become, or are you
what becomes of me? Teach me the wedding parade
that merges the alphabet with my body parts.
Teach me to become a master not an echo.
And wrap me up in your wool, help me
to differ and reach consonance. Give birth to me and I
will give birth to you, sometimes I'm your son, and other times
your father and mother. If you are, I am. If I am, you are.
Call this new time by its foreign names, and host
the distant stranger and life's simple prose
for my poetry to mature. For who, if I utter what isn't poetry,

will understand me? Who will speak to me of a hidden
longing for a lost time if I utter what isn't poetry?
And who will know the stranger's land? . . .

The night became tranquil and complete, a flower
woke up and breathed by the garden fence.

I said to myself: I am witness that I'm still alive
even if from afar. And that I dreamt about the one who had been
dreaming, like me, I dreamt he was I and not another . . .
and that my day, Tuesday, was long and spacious,
and that my night was brief like a short act appended
to a play after the curtains had come down.
Still I won't harm anyone
if I add: It was a beautiful day,
like a true love story aboard an express train.

> If the canary doesn't sing,
> my friend,
> blame only yourself.
> If the canary doesn't sing
> to you, my friend,
> then sing to it . . . sing to it.

II. DENSE FOG OVER THE BRIDGE

My friend asked me, while the fog was dense
over the bridge: Can a thing be known by its opposite?
By dawn, I answered, things will clear up.
He said: But there's no time more dubious than the dawn,
just let your imagination flow with the river:
It's in the blue of dawn, in a prison courtyard
or near a shrubbery of pine, that a young man
optimist with triumph is executed.
And it's in the blue of dawn that the scent of bread
draws a map for life, a spring in summer.
And the dreamers walk lightly, with gaiety
on their dreams' water.
I said: Where then does the dawn take us,
this bridge, where does it take us?
He said: I am not looking for a burial
place. I want a place to live in, to curse it if I please.
I asked, while the place was passing between us
like a gesture: What is place?
He said: The senses' discovery of a foothold
for intuition. Then he sighed:

> The narrow street that used to carry me
> in the spacious evening to her house

in serenity's suburbs
does it still know my heart
like the back of my hand
does it still forget the city smoke?

I said: Don't bet on the realistic,
you won't find the thing alive like its image
waiting for you. Time domesticates
even the mountains, which become higher, or lower
than what you knew them to be,
so where does the bridge take us?
He said: Have we been that long on this road?
I said: Is the fog that dense on the bridge: how
many years have you resembled me?
He said: How many years have you been me?
I said: I don't remember.
He said: I remember only the road.

On the bridge in another country
the saxophone announces the end of winter
and the strangers confess
their blunders when no one sings
along as they sing.

I asked: How long have we been urging the dove
below our nets to fly to the Lotus Tree of Heaven?
He said: I feel I have forgotten my feelings. Soon

we will mimic our voices when we were young, gliding
our *Lam*, lisping our *Seen*, and dozing like a pair of pigeons
on a grapevine that wears the house like a dress. Soon
intuitive life will look upon us. The mountains are still the same
behind their image in my mind. And the ancient sky,
if my imagination hasn't failed me, is still of clear
color and mind, its image is still the same, and the delicious,
pure, beautiful air is also the same, waiting for me
as it has always been.

I said: My friend, the long road has emptied me
of my body. I don't sense its clay or its form.
Whenever I walk I fly. My steps are my vision.
As for my "I" it waves from afar:

> "If this road of yours
> takes too long
> I have work to do in myth."

Divine hands trained us to carve our names
in a willow's index. We were not clear
or mysterious, but our manner
of crossing streets from one epoch to another
raised some questions:

> Who are those
> who stand silently when they see a palm

tree and are quick to prostrate themselves over its shadow?
Who are those who disturb the others
when they laugh?

On the bridge, in another country, he said to me:
Strangers are known by their interrupted stare at the water,
or by their solitary stuttering gait, whereas countrymen
walk toward clear aims in straight paths.
And the stranger circles himself bewildered.

And he said: Each bridge is a rendezvous . . .
On the bridge, I enter
my exterior and surrender my heart
to a palm tree or a sparrow.
I said: Not exactly. On the bridge I walk
to my interior, tame myself,
and attend to its matters. Each bridge is a schism,
so neither are you as you were a while ago
nor are the creatures memories:

> I am two in one
> or am I
> one who is shrapnel in two?
> O bridge
> which of the two
> dispersals am I?

We walked for twenty years on the bridge
we walked for twenty meters on the bridge,
back and forth, and I said: Just a little more to go,
and he said: Just a little more to go,
and together, alone, dreamily we said:

I will walk lightly, my steps on the wind
are an arch that tickles the violin's land,
I will hear my heartbeat in the pebbles
and in the veins of the place.

I will lean my head on a carob trunk,
she's my mother, even if she disowns me.
I'll doze off for a while . . . two little birds will carry me
higher, to a star that has scattered me.

I will waken my soul to a previous ache
forthcoming like a letter from memory's balcony,
and chant: I'm still alive,
I feel the arrow pierce my waist.

I'll look to the right, to the jasmine
where I learned the first songs of the body,
then to the left, to the sea
where I learned fishing for foam.

I will fib like a teenager: This milk
on my pants is the dregs of a dream that troubled me but has passed.
I'll deny that I mimic the long snooze of the Jahili
poet in the eyes of the antelope.

I will drink a fistful of water from a faucet in the garden.
Thirst as water thirsts after itself in longing.
Ask the first passerby: Did you see
a person in the form of a specter searching, like me, for his yesterday?

I will carry my house on my shoulders and walk
as a tortoise walks.
I will hunt a falcon with a broom and ask:
Where is the sin?

I will search mythology and archaeology
and every -ology for my ancient name,
a Canaanite goddess will favor me, she will
swear with lightning: This is my orphaned son.

I will applaud a woman who gave birth to a test-tube
girl who looks nothing like her,
and cry over a man who died
when he heard the gossip.

I will adapt al-Ma'arri's line:
My body is a rag of dust, O weaver of the universe, weave me.

I will write: Creator of Death, leave me
alone for a while . . . let me be.

I will awaken my dead: Sleeping ones! we are equals,
don't you still dream of Resurrection?
I will gather what the winds scattered of Córdoba's love
poems and complete *The Collar of the Dove*.

I will choose from my intimate memories what's fitting:
the scent of wrinkled sheets after making love
is the scent of grass after rain.
I will attest to how the face of stone turns green.

The roses of March will sting me where I was
born the first time.
The pomegranate blossom will bear me then give birth to me
for a final time.

I will move farther from yesterday when I give it back
its inheritance: memory.
I will near tomorrow
when I chase a shrewd lark.

I will know that I am late for my rendezvous
and that my tomorrow
has passed a while ago, as a cloud passes,
without waiting for me.

And that the sky will rain soon
over me
and that I
am walking on the bridge . . .

So, my friend, shouldn't we set foot in the land of story?
It might not be as we imagine, "neither milk
nor honey," and the sky might be ashen,
the dawn blue and dubious. What time is it now?
Is it a bridge that lengthens and shortens, a dawn
that lengthens and schemes? What time is it?

He said: The ancient lands fall asleep behind tourist
citadels. And time migrates in a star
that has singed a romantic horseman. O sleepers
upon memory needles, don't you sense
the sound of earthquakes in a doe's hoof?

I said: Do you have a fever?
But his nightmare persisted: Sleepers! do you not hear
Resurrection hissing in a grain of sand?

I said: Are you talking to me, or yourself?
He said: I have reached the end of the dream . . .
I saw myself as an old man over there, and watched
my heart chase my dog over there
and bark. I saw my bedroom guffaw and ask me:

Are you alive? Come, come and I will carry the air for you
and your wooden cane, the one adorned with Moroccan seashells!
So how will I repeat the beginning, and who am I, my friend?
Who am I without a dream and a woman's company?

I said: Let's visit the crumbs of life, life
as it is, and let's coach ourselves to love things
that used to be ours, and to love things that aren't
ours, yet ours if we look upon them together from a height
like snow falling on a mountain.
Perhaps the mountains are still the same
and the fields are still the same
and life is intuitive and radiant . . .
so shouldn't we enter the land of story?
He said: I'm not looking for a burial place,
I want a place to live in and curse it if I please . . .

He stared at the bridge and said: My friend, this is the door
of truth. We can neither enter nor exit.
And a thing cannot be known by its opposite.
The corridors are shut
and the sky is ashen-faced and narrow,
and dawn's hand is lifting the pants of a woman soldier up high . . .

We remained on the bridge for twenty years
ate canned foods for twenty years
wore the garments of the seasons

and listened to the well-composed new songs
coming out of the soldiers' barracks.
Our sons wed the princesses of exile
who changed their names
and we deserted our destinies to the fans of defeat in the movies
we read our relics over the sand
and were neither mysterious nor clear
like a dawn that yawns a lot.

I asked him: Does the wound still wound you?
He said: I feel nothing. My idea has turned my body into a book
of evidence, nothing proves that I am me
other than a candid death on the bridge.
I gaze at a rose in the faraway and the embers flare,
I gaze at my birthplace behind the distance
and the grave widens.

I said: Don't hasten and don't die now. Life
on the bridge is possible. And metaphor is a spacious vastness.
This, right here, is a limbo between life and the afterlife,
between exile and a neighboring land . . .

He said, while hawks hovered over our heads:
Make of my name your name, tell it about me, live
until the bridge brings you back alive
when tomorrow comes, and don't say I died, or lived near life,
in vain. Say that I looked upon myself from a height,

saw myself wearing trees and was content
with my hand's greeting:

> "If this road takes too long
> then I have work
> to do in myth" . . .

I was alone that day on the bridge,
Christ had just turned ascetic
in a mountain in Jericho's suburbs
before Resurrection.
I was walking, unable to enter
or exit, rotating like a sunflower,
and at night the voice of the night guard woke me.
She was singing to her companion:

> Don't promise me anything
> don't give me
> a rose from Jericho!

III. LIKE A HAND TATTOO IN
THE JAHILI POET'S ODE

I am he, he walks ahead of me and I follow him.
I don't say to him: Right here, right here, a simple thing was ours:
Green stone. Trees. A street. A youthful moon. A reality
no more. He walks ahead of me, and I walk on his shadow in pursuit . . .
whenever he speeds up, shadow rises over the hills,
covers a pine tree in the south, and a willow in the north:
Haven't we already parted? I asked. He said: Indeed!
I offered you imagination's return to the real
and you offered me the apple of gravity.
I said: Where are you taking me then?
He said: Toward the beginning, where you were born,
right here, you and your name.

If it were up to me to bring back the beginning I would
have chosen for my name fewer letters,
easier letters on the foreign woman's ears. March
is the month of storms and emotional yearning.
Spring blooms like a whim in a chat between two,
before a lengthy summer and after a long winter. I remember
only metaphor. I had been barely born
when I noticed a clear resemblance between
the horse's mane and my mother's braids.

Drop metaphor, and take a stroll on the woolly earth, he said.
Sunset brings the stranger back to his well, like a song
that isn't sung, and sunset kindles in us
a longing for a mysterious desire.

Perhaps, perhaps, I said. Everything is an analysis
at sunset. And memories might awaken a calling
that resembles the gesture of death at sunset
or the cadence of a song that isn't sung to anyone:

> Over cypress trees
> east of passion
> there are gilded clouds
> and in the heart a chestnut
> dark-skinned beauty
> diaphanous in shadow
> I drink her like water
> it's time we frolic
> time we travel
> to any planet.

I am he, he walks upon me, and I ask him:
Do you remember anything here?
If you do, ease your tread upon me
because the earth is pregnant with us.

He says: I have seen here in the prairie a bright moon
with a brilliant sorrow like an orange at night

guiding us to the road of wandering.
Without it, mothers wouldn't have found their children.
Without it, the night travelers wouldn't have read
their names suddenly upon the night: "Refugees"
guests of the wind.

My wings were still small for the wind that year . . .
I used to think place was known
by the mothers and the scent of sage. No one
told me this place is called a country,
and that behind the country there were borders, and behind
the borders a place called wandering and exile
for us. I wasn't yet in need of identity . . .
but those who reached us aboard
their combat tanks were transferring the place
in truckloads swiftly away

　　　Place is the passion.

Those are our relics, like a hand tattoo
in the Jahili poet's ode, they pass through us
and we through them — he, the one I once was, said to me
when I didn't know enough words to know the names of our trees
or to call the birds that gather in me by their names.
I wasn't able to memorize the words and protect the place
from being transferred to a strange name fenced in
with eucalyptus trees. While the posters told us:
"You were never here."

Yet the storm softens
and place is the passion.

Those are our relics, the one I once was said . . .
Right here two epochs meet then part, so who are you
in "now's" presence?
I said: Had it not been for the smoke of factories,
I would have said: I am you.
He said: And who are you in yesterday's presence?
I said: Had it not been for the meddling
of the present tense, I would have said: I am we.
He said: And in tomorrow's presence?
I said: I am a love poem you will write when you
yourself choose the myth of love:

    Your skin is wheat color like old harvest songs
    you are dark from the sting of the night
    white from so much laughing water
    when you approach the springs . . .
    your eyes are two almonds
    and two wounds of honey are your lips
    your legs are marble towers
    and on my shoulders your hands are flying birds
    I have a soul you gave me
    fluttering around the place.

Drop metaphor, and walk with me! he said, Do you see
a butterfly trace in the light?

I said: I see you there, I see you passing
like an ancestral notion.
He said: That's how the butterfly recovers
her poetic tasks: a song the astronomers
inscribe only as evidence of eternity's rightness.

Easily I walk upon myself and my shadow
follows. Nothing brings me back
and nothing brings him back,
as if I were someone of me bidding me farewell
in a hurry for his tomorrow.
He tells me: Wait for no one, not even for me.
And I don't bid him farewell.

And it seems like poetry: over the hill
a cloud deceives me, knits its identity around me,
and bequeaths me an orbit I never lose.

    Place has its scent
    sunset has its agonies
    the gazelle has its hunter
    the turtles have their armor for self-defense
    the ants have a kingdom
    the birds have their trysts
    the horses their names
    the wheat its feast
    and as for anthem, the anthem of happy finale
    has no poet.

In the last fraction of life we listen only
to our aching joints or a mosquito droning
like a philosopher who wakes us from sleep.
In the last fraction, we sense the pain
of two amputated legs, as if the feeling reached us late.
We didn't notice our inner wound when we were young,
a wound like an oil painting of a fire that blazes the colors
of our flag and kindles the bull of our anthem.
In the last fraction of life dawn bursts
only because the kindhearted angels
are coerced to perform their tasks . . .

I am he, my self's coachman,
no horse whinnies in my language.

He said: We'll walk even if it is the last fraction
of life, even if the paths let us down.
We'll fly, as a Sufi does, in the words . . . to anywhere.

On a hill high as two heavenly hands we rose
and walked on thorns and holm oak needles,
we blanketed ourselves with the wool of orphaned plants,
united with the dictionary of our names.
I said: Do you feel the poke
of pebbles and the cunning of sand grouse?
He said: I don't feel a thing!
As if feeling is a luxury, as if I am

one adjective of the many absence has.
My life is not with me, it has left me as a woman
leaves a specter-man, she waited
but got bored with waiting, so she guided another
to her feminine treasure ... and if there must be a moon
let it be full, and not a banana horn

I said: You will need some time to know yourself,
so sit on a partition, in between,
because the how is no longer how, and the where is not a where ...

On two heavenly rocks we waited for the sunset
of the gazelle. At sunset the stranger feels
his need to embrace another stranger, at sunset
the two strangers feel a third in their midst: one
who interferes in what they might or might not say ...

    The two of you should bid what was
    and what will be farewell.
    Farewell to the *Nūn* in rhyme
    in the dual name
    and in the purple land!

I said: Who is he?
But an echo answered from afar: I am the realistic one here.
The voice of your destinies. A bulldozer
driver who changed the spontaneity of this place

and cut the braids of your olive trees to match
the soldiers' hair and open a path for the mule
of an ancient prophet. I am the realistic, the tamer of myth.

He is the third of two who sit on two heavenly rocks,
but he doesn't see us as we are:
An old man with a child under his wing, and a child
enmeshed in the old man's wisdom.

We said: Salaam unto man and jinn around us.
He said: I don't get the metaphor.
We said: Why have you infiltrated what we say and what we sense?
He said: The way your shadow wears pebbles
and sand grouse startled me.
We asked: What are you afraid of?
He said: The shadow . . . at times it has the scent of garlic,
other times the scent of blood.
—From where did you come?
—From non-place. For every place
far from God or his land is exile. Who are you?
—We are the grandchildren of the soul of this place.
We were born here, and here we will live if the Lord remains alive.
And every place far from God or his land is exile.
—The way your shadow wears the place raises suspicion.
—What do you suspect?
—A shadow struggling with another shadow?
—Is it because the distance between yesterday
and our present remains fertile for the trinity of time?

—It was yesterday that I killed you.
—Death pardoned us.
—I am eternity's watchman, he shouted:
 Say farewell to what was
 and what will be
 say farewell to the scent of garlic
 and blood in the shadow of this place ...

But what's the meaning of this thing,
this thing that makes me
a self then gives back to meaning its features?
How am I born from a thing I later make?

I extend in the high trees and the thing raises me
to heaven, I become a cautious bird
that nothing deceives or obliterates.

In each thing I see my soul, and what I cannot feel hurts me.
And what doesn't feel the hurt my soul causes it also hurts me.

I and I don't believe in this dirt road, yet we walk trailing the ant line
(tracking is the map of instinct). And neither has the sun
completely set, nor has the orange moon become fully lit.

I and I don't believe the beginning
waits for those who return to it, like a mother on the house's doorstep.
Yet we walk even if the sky fails us.

I and I don't believe the story
brought us back as two witnesses to what we had done:
I forgot about you like my cherry-stained shirt
when you ran into a forest and became filled with regret.
And I, too, forgot about you when you kept a phoenix
feather and became filled with regret.

Shall we make amends then? I asked him.
He said: Hold on. There, two meters away from us,
is my school, let's go and rescue the alphabet
from the spiderweb, though we'll leave for it the weeping vowels!
I remember it, I said: Two ancient walls without a ceiling
like two letters of a language distorted by sand
and by a Sodom-like earthquake. Fat cows sleeping over the alphabet.
A dog wagging the tail of mirth and content. And a small night
readying its things for the bustle of foxes.
He said: Life always continues its custom after us.
What a thing! What a shameless thing
life is, it only thinks of fulfilling its desires.
I said: Shall we make amends then and share
this absence? We are here alone in the poem.
He said: Hold on. There, on the edge of the hill,
on the east side, lies the family's graveyard.
Let's go before the dark descends over the dead
and bid salaam unto the sleeping,
those who dream of their paradise garden
safe and sound: salaam unto the lightly ascending
on the ladder of God.

In the presence of death we grasp only the accuracy of our names . . .
A lewd absurdity. We found not one stone
that carries a victim's name, not my name or yours.
Which of the two of us died, I asked, I or I?

He said: I don't know anymore.
I said: Shall we make amends?
He said: Hold on!
I said: Is this the return we have always desired?
He said: And a comedy by one of our frivolous goddesses,
have you enjoyed the visit thus far?
I said: Is this the end of your exile?
He said: And the beginning of yours.
I said: What's the difference?
He said: The cunning of eloquence.
I said: Eloquence isn't necessary for defeat.
He said: Yes it is. Eloquence convinces a widow
to marry a foreign tourist, eloquence protects
the roses of the garden from the absurdity of the wind.
—Then let's make amends?
—If the dead and the living sign, in one body, a truce.
—Here I am, the dead and the living.
—I forgot you, who are you?
—I am your "I," its duplicate, your "I" that noticed what
the butterfly said to me: O my brother in fragility . . .
He said: But the butterfly has already burned.
—Then don't burn as it has.

And I turned toward him but didn't see him, so I screamed
with all my strength: Wait, wait for me! Take everything
from me except my name.

He didn't wait for me, he flew away . . .
Then the night reached me, and my shout drew
a specter passing by.

I said: Who are you?
He said: Salaam unto you. I said: And unto you,
who are you?

He said: I am a foreign tourist who loves your myths.
And I would love to marry one of Anat's widowed daughters!

IV. COUNTERPOINT

FOR EDWARD SAID

New York, November, Fifth Avenue,
the sun a shattered metal saucer,
I said to my estranged self in the shade:
Is this Sodom or Babylon?

There, at the door of an electric abyss
high as the sky, I met Edward
thirty years ago, time was less defiant then.
And we each said: If your past is experience
make your tomorrow meaning and vision!
Let's go to our tomorrow certain
of imagination's candor, and of the miracle of grass.

I don't recall that we went to the movies
that evening, but I heard ancient Indians calling me:
Trust neither the horse nor modernity.

No, no victim asks his torturer:
Are you me? If my sword were bigger
than my rose, would you wonder
whether I would act similarly?

A question like this piques the curiosity of the novelist
in a glass-walled office overlooking some irises in the garden . . .
where the hypothetical hand is as white as the novelist's
conscience when he settles his account
with the human instinct: There's no tomorrow
in yesterday, onward then . . .

Though progress might be the bridge of return
to barbarity . . .

New York. Edward wakes to a sluggish
dawn. Plays a Mozart piece. Runs around
in the university tennis court. Thinks
of the migration of birds over borders and checkpoints.
Reads *The New York Times*. Writes his tense
commentary. Damns an orientalist who guides a general
to the weakness in the heart of a woman from the East.
Showers. Chooses his suit with a rooster's elegance.
Drinks his coffee with cream. Screams
at the dawn: Come on, don't procrastinate!

On the wind he walks. And on the wind
he knows who he is. There's no ceiling for the wind
and no house. The wind is a compass
to the stranger's north.

He says: I am from there, I am from here,
but I am neither there nor here.
I have two names that meet and part,
and I have two languages, I forget
with which I dream. For writing I have
an English with obedient vocabulary,
and I have a language of heaven's dialogue
with Jerusalem, it has a silver timbre
but it doesn't obey my imagination.

And Identity? I asked.
He said: Self-defense . . .
Identity is the daughter of birth, but in the end
she's what her owner creates, not an inheritance
of a past. I am the plural. Within my interior
my renewing exterior resides . . . yet I
belong to the victim's question. Were I not
from there I would have trained my heart
to rear the gazelle of metonymy,
so carry your land wherever you go,
and be a narcissist if you need to be.

I asked: The outside world is an exile
and the inside world is an exile
so who are you between the two?
I don't completely know myself

lest I lose myself, he said. I am what I am
and I am my other in a duality that finds
harmony between speech and gesture.
And if I were a poet I would have said:

> I am two in one
> like a sparrow's wings,
> and if spring is late
> I stay content with bearing
> the good omen.

He loves a land then departs from it.
(Is the impossible far?)
He loves departure to anything.
In free travel between cultures, the researchers
of human essence might find enough seats
for everyone. Here is a periphery advancing.
Or a center receding. The East is not completely East
and the West is not completely West.
Because identity is open to plurality,
it isn't a citadel or a trench.

Metaphor was asleep on the riverbank
and were it not for pollution
it would have embraced the other bank. I asked:
Have you written a novel?

I tried, he said . . . I tried to bring back my image
in the mirrors of faraway women,
but they had already infiltrated their fortified nights
and said: We have a world separate from text.
Man will not write woman, the riddle-and-dream.
Woman will not write man, the symbol-and-star.
No love resembles another love.
No night resembles another night.
Let's enumerate the traits of men and laugh.

—So what did you do?
—I laughed at my absurdity
and threw the novel in the trash!

The intellectual reins in the novelist's rendition
and the philosopher dissects the singer's rose.

He loves a land then departs from it
and says: I am what I become and will become.
I will make myself by myself
and choose my exile.
My exile is the backdrop of the epic scene,
I defend the poets' need
to join tomorrow with memories,
I defend trees the birds wear
as country and exile.

I defend a moon still fit for a poem of love.
I defend an idea fractured by its owner's fragility
and a land the myths have kidnapped.

—Can you return to anything?
—What's ahead of me drags what's behind me in a hurry . . .
there's no time in my wristwatch for me to write down lines
on the sand, but I can visit yesterday, like strangers do,
when they listen in the evening to a pastoral poet:

> A girl by the spring fills her jug
> with the milk of clouds
> she laughs and cries from a bee that stung
> her heart in the wind-rise
> of absence. Is love what aches the water
> or is it an ailment in fog . . . ?
>   etc., etc.

—Then you are prone to the affliction of longing?
—A longing for tomorrow is farther and higher.
My dream leads my steps. And my vision
seats my dream on my knees like a cat.
My dream is the realistic imaginary and the son of will:

> We are able
> to alter
> the inevitability of the abyss!

—And what of longing for yesterday?
—A sentiment that doesn't concern the intellectual except
to comprehend a stranger's yearning to the tools of absence.
My longing is a conflict over a present
that grabs tomorrow by the testicles.

—But didn't you sneak to yesterday when you went
to the house, your house, in al-Talbiah, in Jerusalem?
—I prepared myself to stretch out in my mother's bed
as a child does when he's scared
of his father. And I tried to retrieve my birth
and trace the Milky Way on the roof of my old house, I tried
to palpate the skin of absence and smell summer
in the jasmine garden. But the beast of truth
distanced me from a longing that was looking over
my shoulder like a thief.

—Were you frightened? What frightened you?
—I couldn't meet loss face-to-face.
I stood like a beggar at the doorstep.
Do I ask permission, from strangers who sleep
in my own bed, to visit myself for five minutes? Do I
bow respectfully to those who reside in my childhood dream?
Would they ask: Who is this inquisitive foreign visitor?
Would I be able to talk about war and peace
between the victims and the victims
of victims without interruption? Would they
say to me: There's no place for two dreams in one bed?

He's neither himself nor me
he's a reader wondering what poetry
can tell us in the age of catastrophe.

Blood
      and blood
            and blood
                    in your land,
in my name and yours, in the almond
blossom, in the banana peel, in the infant's
milk, in light and shadow,
in wheat grains, in the salt container.
Proficient snipers hit their marks
with excellence
            and blood
                and blood
                    and blood . . .

This land is smaller than the blood of its offspring
who stand on the threshold of Resurrection like offerings.
Is this land really
blessed or baptized
          in blood
              and blood
                and blood
that doesn't dry up with prayer or sand?
No justice in the pages of this holy book

suffices for the martyrs to celebrate the freedom
of walking on clouds. Blood in daylight.
Blood in the dark. Blood in the words.
But he says: The poem might host defeat
like a thread of light that glistens in a guitar's heart.
Or as a Christ on a mare laden with beautiful
metaphor. Aesthetic is only the presence
of the real in form.

In a world without sky, land becomes
an abyss. And the poem, one of condolence's gifts.
And an adjective of wind: northern or southern.
Don't describe what the camera sees of your wounds
and scream to hear yourself, to know
that you're still alive, and that life
on this earth is possible. Invent a wish
for speech, devise a direction or a mirage
to prolong the hope, and sing.
Aesthetic is a freedom.

I said: A life that is defined only
in antithesis to death . . . isn't a life!

He said: We will live, even if life abandons us
to ourselves. Let's become the masters of words
that will immortalize their readers—
as your brilliant friend Ritsos said.

Then he said: If I die before you do,
I entrust you with the impossible!
I asked: Is the impossible far?
He said: As far as one generation.
—And what if I die before you do?
He said: I will console Galilee's mountains
and write: Aesthetic is only the attainment
of the suitable. Now don't forget: If I die before you do,
I entrust you with the impossible.

When I visited him in the new Sodom,
in 2002, he was struggling against
Sodom's war on the Babylonians,
and against cancer.
He was like the last epic hero
defending Troy's right
to share in the narrative.

A falcon
bids his summit farewell
and soars higher and higher . . .
residing over Olympus
and other summits
produces boredom.

Farewell,
farewell to the poem
of pain.

NOTES

GLOSSARY

NOTES

The Tragedy of Narcissus the Comedy of Silver

36 The quotation "Behold, Saladin, we have returned . . ." is attributed to the French general Henri Gouraud upon conquering Damascus in 1920 and while standing over Saladin's grave.

Mural

104 The quotation "a stranger is another stranger's brother" is a paraphrase of the infamous hemistich in a poem of Imru' el-Qyss, where he says: "Each stranger is another stranger's kin."

115 "The clarity of shadows in synonyms" (not to mention the original lyricism) is a certain shortcoming in fully translating the dimensions of Darwish's poetry.

128 The quotation "I did not bear a boy to bear his father's death" is a paraphrase of a famous stanza of al-Ma'arri (see note on al-Ma'arri below): "This is what my father committed against me and I've committed it against no one."

134 The metaphor "gripping the wind" belongs to the legendary Arab poet al-Mutanabbi (Ahmad bin Hussein, 915–965).

144 *Meem, Hā, Wāw, Dal* are the twenty-fourth, sixth, twenty-seventh, and eighth letters of the Arabic alphabet and make up the poet's name. In the Arabic text all the words listed after each letter are alliterations (to say the least) of that letter; this effect is impossible to duplicate in translation.

GLOSSARY

Aba: a traditional robelike garment.

Aegean Sea: likely a reference to a presumed origin of the Philistine tribes, one of the Sea People.

Aghwar: the lowland of the Jordan Valley. The reference in *Mural* is to the biblical encounter Jesus had with the devil there.

Aleph: the first letter in the Arabic alphabet.

Anat: a principal Canaanite goddess of love, war, and fertility (see *Baal*).

al-Attar, Farid al-Din: a twelfth-century Persian Sufi theoretician, who was born in Nishapur in 1142. He is the author of *Conference of the Birds* (written in 1177), on which "The Hoopoe" is based.

Azaan: the call to prayer (from which "muezzin" is derived).

Baal: a principal Canaanite god. Both Anat and Baal were initially incorporated into early Hebraic tradition. (See also Darwish's usage of "the Torah of the roots" and "the buried Torah of Canaan" in "Take Care of the Stags, Father" and "The Tragedy of Narcissus the Comedy of Silver," respectively.)

Barada: a river that runs through Damascus.

Bowaib: a place in southern Iraq near the birthplace of Badr Shakir al-Sayyab (1926–64), father of the modern Arabic poem. The great contemporary Iraqi poet Saadi Yussef, a close friend of Mahmoud Darwish, also hails from this region.

al-Buhturi (821–897): a classical Arab poet, born in Syria, who lived most of his life in Baghdad during the reign of al-Mutawakkil, an Abbasid caliph.

Cana in Galilee: the place where Jesus turned water into wine.

The Collar of the Dove (or *Ring of the Dove*): a treatise on art and love by Ibn Hazm, an influential eleventh-century Arab Andalusian philosopher.

Damascus Road: the road to Damascus on which Saul, on his way to annihilate Christians, received visions, converted to Christianity, and became the Apostle Paul.

Dhād: the fifteenth letter in the Arabic alphabet. A sound unique to the language that has come to signify it.

Edward Said (1935–2003): a Palestinian-American literary theorist, cultural critic, political activist, and a founding figure of postcolonial theory.

Enkidu: a wild creature and friend of Gilgamesh in the epic of *Gilgamesh*. Enkidu helped his friend slay the Bull of Heaven and, as a consequence, was punished by the gods with death. Gilgamesh's grief over the loss of his friend is perhaps the first documented narrative of human burial.

Ghazan-Arghun: a thirteenth-century Mongolian ruler whose seat of power was in Iran. He eventually converted to Islam.

Gilgamesh: the hero of the Sumerian epic poem *Gilgamesh*, which is probably the earliest documented narrative fiction about immortality and creation.

Hajj: the annual Muslim pilgrimage to Mecca.

Hejaz: the region where Mecca lies in modern-day Saudi Arabia.

Hulagu (1217–1265): a grandson of Genghis Khan, responsible for the destruction of Baghdad in 1258 and the brutal subjugation of the region. "The grand death / in Tigris" recalls the river's ink color after the libraries in Baghdad were destroyed and dead bodies jammed the water.

Hyksos: an Asiatic people who invaded ancient Egypt in the seventeenth century B.C.E.

Ibn Khaldun: an Arab scholar who lived in the fourteenth century and is most known for his *Muqaddimah* (Introduction or Prolegomenon), which is credited as the foundation of the modern-day disciplines of social sciences.

Ibn Rushd (Averroës, 1126–1198): an Arab, Muslim, Andalusian philosopher, physician, and scholar, often regarded in Western Europe as an early influence on secular thought.

Ibn Sina (Avicenna, 980–1037): a Muslim physician, philosopher, and scholar known for many treatises on logic and medicine that were vital to the European Renaissance.

Imru' el-Qyss (500–540?): one of the seven pre-Islamic (Jahili) poets whose odes were celebrated and presumably suspended (see *mu'allaqah*) on the walls of the Kaaba in Mecca. Imru' el-Qyss was a prince of Kindah who led a life of sensual pleasure, but when he failed to avenge the murder of his father, the king, he traveled to Constantinople to ask the Byzantine emperor for help (hence "the path to Caesar"). He was placated with the nominal governance of Palestine but died shortly thereafter of an ulcerative skin disease rumored to have been the result of poison placed inside his aba (robe).

Intaba: an herb often used as tea.

Jahili: pre-Islamic.

Khosrau: title of pre-Islamic Persian kings.

Kurd commander: Saladin (see his entry).

Lablab: an easy-growing, drought-tolerant, flowery twining vine with edible seeds.

Lam: the twenty-third letter of the Arabic alphabet, equivalent to *L* in English.

Lotus Tree of Heaven: Sidrat al-Muntaha, the highest degree of attainment, is a fantastic tree that arises from the Seventh Heaven and reaches God's throne.

al-Ma'arri, Abul-Ala' (973–1057): a great Arab poet and philosopher who became blind as a child after contracting smallpox. He was known for his satire and humanism. An early advocate of experiment in prosody, he was the first Arab poet to compose a cohesive, thematic poetry collection. He is also known for *Risalat al-Ghufran* (The Treatise of Forgiveness), which is likely to have influenced Dante's *Divine Comedy*. Al-Ma'arri is mentioned or alluded to on several occasions in *If I Were Another*.

Majnoon Laila: Qyss Ibn el-Mulawah is known primarily by his beloved's name, as Qyss Laila or Majnun Laila. He and Laila were lovers in the seventh century. But the unrequited love drove Qyss to madness (and brilliant poetry), and he died a wanderer in the desert.

Mizmar: a wind instrument resembling the oboe.

Mu'allaqah: a suspended or hung poem; denotes any of the famous seven pre-Islamic odes that were hung on the walls of the Kaaba in Mecca and memorized in the hearts and minds of the faithful (see *Imru' el-Qyss* and *Tarafah*).

Muwashah: a form of Arabic poetry, often set to song, prevalent since the days of the Andalus and still popular today.

Nahawand: one of the scales in Arabic music.

Nairuz: the Persian New Year, in spring.

Negus: the title of ancient Ethiopian kings.

Nineveh: a great Assyrian city on the eastern bank of the Tigris, center of Ishtar worship and part of the biblical narrative of Jonah.

Nishapur: a town in Iran strategically located on the Silk Road acting as gateway of the Mediterranean to China. It was a world cultural center in the twelfth century and the birthplace of the influential Sufi thinker Farid Addin al-Attar (see his entry).

Nūn: the twenty-fifth letter in the Arabic alphabet, with multiple functions as prefix, suffix, and diacritical mark. Its musical ring affected Darwish, beginning in childhood.

Oud: an Arabic stringed instrument comparable to the lute or the guitar.

Passion's Wadi: the second of seven wadis on the road to attainment in the narrative *Conference of the Birds* (see *al-Attar*).

Purple (thread or land): refers to Tyrian purple, *urjuwan*, a nonfading dye made from snails, a luxury trade item discovered and distributed by the Phoenicians during Roman times. The Phoenicians were a Canaanite people who established an important maritime civilization that advanced the use of the alphabet throughout the old world.

Quraish: the tribe of the prophet Mohammad in Mecca.

Rababa: a stringed instrument resembling a fiddle.

Rasafah: a neighborhood in Baghdad, on the eastern bank of the Tigris, and probably the oldest in the city's Arab-Muslim history. It was central during the Abbasid reign, and houses al-Muntassiriyeh, one of the oldest universities in the region, established in the tenth century. The infamous Mutannabi Street is located there.

Saladin, Salahuddin al-Ayyubi (1137–1193): a Muslim Kurd leader who resisted the Crusades and recaptured Jerusalem in 1187. He was also known for his magnanimity toward his foes.

Samarkand: a city in modern-day Uzbekistan that dates to before Alexander the Great, who conquered it. In the eighth century, Muslim Arabs established it as a cultural center; it was destroyed by the Mongol invasion in the thirteenth century.

Seen: the twelfth letter of the Arabic alphabet, equivalent to S in English.

Shulamit: the beloved woman in the Song of Songs.

Suhrwardi, Shihab al-Din (1155–1191): a Persian Sufi Muslim philosopher, founder of the School of Illumination (Ishraq), a concept that recurs in Darwish's later poems.

Surat al-Rahman: the chapter (or sura) of the Compassionate (one of God's ninety-nine names) is the fifty-fifth in the Quran. Most of its verses end in the letter *Nūn*. The sura is also significant because the speaker addresses two selves, thus heightening the mysticism of identity, a concept well developed in Sufi literature, as in Darwish's "I." (See also Darwish's poem "Like the Nūn in Surat al-Rahman," 1996, dedicated to his grandfather.)

Tarafah Ibn al-Abd: a sixth-century, Arab, pre-Islamic poet and one of the authors of the seven hanging odes in the Kaaba (see *mu'allaqah*). He was a brilliant young poet, killed when he was twenty years old.

Tatars: a central Asiatic people who formed part of the Mongolian invasion and destruction of the Levant in the thirteenth century.

Throne verse: a famous verse in the Quran that describes the vastness of God and his seat in the universe.

Two-horned King: a mysterious reference in the Quran, probably to Alexander the Great.

Wadi of Knowledge: the third wadi on the road to attainment in *Conference of the Birds* (see *al-Attar*).

Ya': the twenty-eighth and last letter of the Arabic alphabet and one of its three vowels.

Zanzalakht: the chinaberry tree or Persian lilac, an abundant shade tree in the Galilee.

Zaradasht: Zarathustra.

Zizyphus: jujube.

MAHMOUD DARWISH was born in the village of al-Birweh in Galilee, Palestine, on March 13, 1941. His family was forced to flee to Lebanon when he was six years old, but they returned after the creation of Israel in 1948. Darwish remained in Israel until 1970, when, having been jailed several times for his poetry and activism, he decided to leave Haifa for Moscow. He later lived in Cairo and by 1973 had moved to Beirut, where he became the cultural editor of *Palestinian Affairs* and, later, the editor of the internationally acclaimed literary journal *al-Karmel*. After the Israeli invasion of Lebanon in 1982, he moved to Tunis, and then to Paris, where he settled for more than a decade until his return to Ramallah in 1996. During his years in Paris, where he published all the works of his middle period, Darwish was recognized as a world poet. In the last twelve years of his life, he divided his time between Amman and Ramallah.

Darwish wrote more than twenty books of poetry and ten of prose. His work has been translated into nearly thirty languages. Among his numerous honors are the Chevalier of the Order of Arts and Letters, the Lannan Cultural Freedom Award, the Prins Claus Award (Holland), the Golden Wreath (Macedonia), the Ibn Sina Prize, the Lotus Prize, and an honorary doctorate in philosophy from the University of Chile. He died in Houston, Texas, on August 9, 2008, after complications from cardiovascular surgery.

FADY JOUDAH's previous translation of Mahmoud Darwish's poetry, *The Butterfly's Burden*, won a TLS Translation Prize (the Saif Ghobash–Banipal Prize) for Arabic Literary Translation from the Society of Authors in the UK. His first poetry collection, *The Earth in the Attic*, was published in the Yale Series of Younger Poets in 2008. He lives in Houston, Texas.